How to go Carbon Neutral

How to go Carbon Neutral

A practical guide to treading more lightly upon the Earth

Mark Brassington

howto**books**

Published by How To Books Ltd,
Spring Hill House, Spring Hill Road,
Begbroke , Oxford OX5 1RX, United Kingdom
Tel: (01865) 375794, Fax: (01865) 379162
info@howtobooks.co.uk
www.howtobooks.co.uk

How To Books greatly reduce the carbon footprint of their books by
sourcing their typesetting and printing in the UK.

British Library Cataloguing in Publication Data
A catalogue record for this book is available from the British Library

ISBN 978 1 84528 250 9

Cover design by Baseline Arts Ltd, Oxford
Produced for How To Books by Deer Park Productions, Tavistock
Typeset by Pantek Arts Ltd, Maidstone, Kent.
Printed and bound by Cromwell Press Ltd, Trowbridge, Wiltshire

NOTE: The material contained in this book is set out in good faith for
general guidance and no liability can be accepted for loss or expense
incurred as a result of relying in particular circumstances on statements
made in the book. Laws and regulations are complex and liable to change,
and readers should check the current position with the relevant authorities
before making personal arrangements.

Contents

Earth at Breaking Point

'Today's mighty oak is just yesterday's nut that held its ground.'

Anon

POPULATION OVERLOAD

Before oil and gas came along, the earth could only support about 1.5 billion people. It simply wasn't possible to feed any more than that. But that was before oil. Today, our world is awash with cheap oil and has been for over 40 years. In 1950, world production of oil was around three billion barrels per year. Today it is around 30. This has meant that, using oil and gas, we can almost literally *make* food. This has allowed our population to blaze out of control to over seven billion people and rising, far more than this tiny planet can support. There are more people alive today than have ever lived in the entire history of the planet.

This has created some problems.

The first major problem is the sheer pressure that this has created on our planet, on our environment. You only have to drive around rural England for a short while to see how little land there is left for nature. People no longer live in harmony with nature; we have encroached on it for living space. We have failed to keep our numbers in check, and nature has paid the price. She has been tarmacked over and strip-mined to support our staggering numbers.

GLOBAL WARMING

This is the second problem.

While this book was being written, an ice shelf the size of London broke free from Canada and started drifting around the Arctic ocean. The shockwaves of this titanic shift were felt by earthquake monitors 250 miles away. If it collided with an oil rig, it would be like a fly hitting your windscreen. That ice shelf formed between 3,000 and 4,500 years ago, and only now has it snapped off. The first cracks started appearing in the 1970s, but it wasn't until now that it reached breaking point.

Global warming has been directly created by the feast at the fossil fuel table which has created the extremes of weather we are beginning to see, such as the droughts which have wiped out harvests across Europe. As the years pass, the cost of such 'natural' disasters is stacking up, especially for insurers.

We have even seen an entire city swallowed up – New Orleans. This was caused by an immense hurricane, which was directly attributable to the excessively high temperatures of the seas. In pre-industrial times, the destruction of an entire city would have been cause for deep concern around the world – panic in fact. Today, it is just another news story, and the actions which caused it continue unchecked. The point to notice here is that global warming is not just due to fossil fuels, but also to an unchecked population, which is a result of fossil fuel gluttony.

THE END OF THE OIL AGE

'The idea of the lights going out is not a fantasy. People seem to accept that security of energy supply is a right. It is not.'

Simon Skilling, director of strategy and energy policy at Eon UK

The third problem is where fossil fuel and our population meet – 'peak oil'.

The whole of Western society runs on oil. It's not just cars, buses and trains which use it, but all plastics and many chemicals and materials are made from oil. If oil suddenly disappeared from the face of the planet, we would be plunged into a new dark age overnight. And oil is already disappearing – we are at, or nearing, the halfway point, which is called peak oil.

We are not talking about oil running out overnight, but a radical increase in scarcity and cost. Since 2004 oil has been rising an average $13/barrel each year. At this rate we will break the $100 mark some time in 2008. This has huge implications – oil is not just used to power cars, but also to grow food. So dependent are we on oil for food production that in the US it takes 10 calories of fossil fuel to make one calorie of food. Food is transported over thousands of miles before it reaches our plates, often by air travel. In addition, modern fertiliser is made from natural gas – another fossil fuel.

In addition to our food, oil is required in manufacture of all plastics, computers, high-tech gadgets, medicine, even our water supply. Without oil, and other fossil fuels, western society will be reduced to a shadow of its self.

This is the serious and sharp end of carbon emissions and it is coming soon to an empty supermarket shelf near you. This is the consequence of not bothering. If you want to know more about peak oil, then buckle your seatbelts and head over to www.lifeaftertheoilcrash.net and www.peakoil.com

THE SOLUTION

'You must be the change you want to see in the world.'

Mahatma Gandhi

This bandwagon's getting crowded

It's impossible to pick up a newspaper these days without seeing an article about global warming. In the UK Climate Bill, the government set the ambitious target of reducing carbon emissions by 60 per cent by 2050. Everywhere you look there are articles about businesses embracing green technologies. Even the supermarkets, the stereotypical villains of the marketplace, are now proclaiming ambitious goals, and branding themselves 'green'. Marks and Spencer are aiming to be carbon neutral by 2012, Asda has set a target of zero waste by 2010, and Tesco has plans to put the carbon footprint on the label of all their products.

But are they really serious, or is this all just greenwash? Are these targets feasible? Or even possible?

Promises that can't be kept

There are tremendous savings to be made in carbon emissions in just about every area of life, and businesses are no different. In fact, for businesses, there are even more options available because they have the capital to invest and operate on a large scale. But despite the opportunities that businesses and governments have, and these melodramatic goals, there are no signs that any of them will ever be met. Renewable technologies require investment and hardship, and this isn't happening.

It would require deeply unpopular policies to cut Britain's emissions by 60 per cent. Air travel would be practically banned and car travel would have to be rationed to a tiny fraction, with the majority of travellers on buses. Supermarkets would be going out of business because no one would be able to drive to them anymore. Millions of houses would be converted over to wood fuel, with thousands of acres of trees being planted to supply the demand for fuel. The evidence would be everywhere in our lives. But it isn't happening. Instead, the M1 is being widened by an extra lane.

If big businesses were to become carbon neutral, they would have to source a massive proportion of their goods locally, which would mean a radical increase in price, which would put them at a big disadvantage with their competitors. And we are only talking about direct energy here. If you were to count embodied energy, these businesses would not be able to use or sell anything made of plastic or metal or glass. They would have to source any additional computers second-hand! Obviously, this isn't happening, and it is unlikely to ever happen until the fossil fuel bonanza finally winds down.

If you want something done properly...

The only way we can become carbon neutral in the foreseeable future is on a personal, voluntary basis. Despite all the big speeches, business and government have little intention of going carbon neutral beyond superficial measures to boost their image. They each have interests to protect, and curbing emissions would severely damage those interests. It is up to us as individuals to go carbon neutral.

Many books look at how governments 'ought' to act to prevent global warming, or how businesses are behaving irresponsibly to cause emissions, but really it is us who vote for these governments, and us who give these businesses our money. We cannot escape this personal accountability.

BREAKING THE ADDICTION

When you look at how our lives are dominated by oil and other fossil fuels, it can be quite daunting to try and free yourself from this immense dependency. Our whole society is structured so that fossil fuels are an assumption.

So how can anyone become carbon neutral?

There are several books out there with hundreds of suggestions for reducing your carbon emissions. The aim of this book is to teach you the *underlying principles* of personal carbon emissions, and show you how they can be reduced or eradicated, rather than offering a mixed bag of hints and tips. If the whole subject seems too big, then simply start with one thing, such as food, or heat. Composting and insulation are cheap and very effective.

As the old saying goes, 'success is a journey, not a destination'. There's no need to beat yourself up just because you're still driving to work, for example, as long as you are on the journey to sustainability. What matters is that you have a plan to move yourself towards becoming more carbon neutral. That plan may take years, decades, maybe a lifetime to complete, but as long as you are making daily progress towards your eventual goal, that is what counts.

MOVING FORWARDS

You may already be well down the path towards becoming carbon neutral. Maybe you already recycle and compost, and now you want to move on to a more ambitious project, such as installing solar hot water, or switching your gas central heating to a wood stove. These are the inputs of going carbon neutral and often involve a substantial investment. It can take quite a while to save up, but that needn't be an obstacle. For managing personal finance I can recommend no better book than *The Richest Man in Babylon* by George S Clason.

Maintaining motivation is all important – keep a graph on the kitchen wall where the whole family can see it showing how much money has been saved so far, so everyone knows how close you are to the next step. And remember, when you convert a part of your life away from fossil fuel dependency, it is not an expense, *it is an investment*. This investment will pay off not just for you, but for future generations as well.

Get the whole family involved in your project. Children can help too – picking blackberries, making jam, recycling, watering the garden – whatever it takes. In fact children are often the most enthusiastic! After all, they are the ones who will have to live in the world that's left behind, after our thirst for energy has run its course.

GOING CARBON NEUTRAL IN THE COMMUNITY

Beyond yourself and your family, you can look to help people in your local community. Perhaps you'd like to help the local school get a wind turbine, or plant fruiting trees around your local area – helping to absorb carbon and reduce food miles.

There are plenty of people around like you, who would like to change their lives towards becoming more carbon neutral. If you would like to form a group of like-minded people with a view to becoming carbon neutral, then you will be glad to know that there is already an organisation set up to help you do just this.

Global Action Plan (www.globalactionplan.org.uk, telephone: 020 7405 5633) runs a scheme around the UK, helping people set up local Eco Teams. These run for a short period of time, in which each member of the team sets their own goals for reducing their carbon footprint, be it through recycling, reducing car use, heat insulation or anything you like. Meetings are held each month to record measurements and discuss any issues, then at the end of the Eco Team's time, you can see what difference you've made. Of course, some changes are easier to measure than others! Alternatively you could set up your own scheme in your local area, such as a campaign to set up a wind turbine, or a car sharing scheme.

Your action counts

Finally, whether it is through concern for the damage caused by global warming, or out of a desire to protect yourself and your family from Britain's impending energy crisis, reducing carbon emissions can only be a good thing. Many people think that their actions are too small to have any effect, when compared with the scale of coal burning in China, for example. While it is true that a single person's actions have little power, it is important to remember that you are not a single person; you are a member of a huge, international movement. Saying that a person's actions don't matter is like saying a person's vote doesn't matter. Every time you buy an item, or travel somewhere, you are making a vote for a certain way of life. When you change your actions, you change your vote. Even the act of saving up for a solar panel is significant, because you are withdrawing money from other areas, and so you are withdrawing your vote.

Your actions do matter.

If you are still in doubt, then answer this: why are the supermarkets suddenly going green? Have they suddenly gained a conscience? I don't think so. They are responding to the actions and opinions of their customers. It is the actions and opinions of us all that shape the world around us, and it can be quite liberating to realise how much power you really do have over your environment. Small actions now can plant seeds for the future.

CHANGING YOUR LIFE

But most of all, when you change the way you live your life, you make it easier for other people to change their lives. By setting a positive example, you show that it can be done, and this makes it socially safer for others to do so. This in turn sends signals to government as part of a movement, that some people are willing to accept the harsher measures that will be needed to make the shift, such as higher taxes on air travel, or even rationing. It shows that there is a groundswell of public opinion that wants to go carbon neutral, and to power down. It isn't just your vote that shapes the government, it is your actions *between* those elections, and those actions matter far more than you probably realise.

It's your life. Make it count.

Getting Started

WHAT IS CARBON NEUTRAL?

When we talk of being carbon neutral, we are talking of our actions not contributing any carbon dioxide (CO_2) to the atmosphere. CO_2 is a greenhouse gas that contributes to global warming, a growing problem on our planet. So being carbon neutral is about not contributing to the ongoing problem of global warming. It is about recognising the problem, then gradually drawing away from the cause.

We are simplifying matters by only looking at CO_2 and being carbon neutral, as there are other greenhouse gases, and some of them are even more damaging than CO_2. These include methane (CH_4), typically from agriculture and landfill, and nitrous oxide (N_2O), also mainly from agriculture. But broadly speaking, if we aim to take the measures outlined in this book, our efforts will help reduce the production of these gases as well.

The Sources of carbon

So where does all this carbon, or CO_2, come from? The first thing that usually springs to mind when we talk about the problem of carbon emissions is pollution – like driving cars, or power stations belching dirty smoke into the atmosphere. But carbon emissions come from a variety of sources, and although opinion seems to be divided on the magnitude of these sources, what does seem to be a consensus is that 'around half UK CO_2 emissions come from industry and commerce, supporting our everyday lifestyle' (National Energy Foundation: www.nef.org.uk). So although much of the carbon is produced by businesses over which we have little influence, around half of all the carbon produced is done so *by us*. This means that by taking personal responsibility for the carbon we produce we can each make a tremendous difference. According to Coinet (Climate Outreach & Information Network: coinet.org.uk), our personal carbon contributions come from the following sources:

air travel	34%
gas	27%
car	19%
electricity	16%
bus	2%
rail	2%.

Simply speaking, our carbon emissions are connected mainly to our *energy use*: how much of it we use and how 'dirty' that energy is.

Off-setting

There is a lot of talk at the moment about 'off-setting' your carbon emissions. Off- setting centres around the carbon cycle – that as carbon is emitted, it is also absorbed. Wood, for example, is burned, which produces carbon dioxide, which is then eventually absorbed back into new trees. Carbon is emitted from a 'carbon source', and absorbed back into a 'carbon sink'.

The argument of the 'off-setter' runs like this: I can drive my big car because I'm dedicating these six trees as carbon sinks, which will absorb the equivalent carbon produced, and so 'offset' my big car. I don't buy this. Within a generation or two there won't be any affordable oil left, let alone any big cars! *Burning fossil fuels is not a part of the carbon cycle.*

As Rob Newman says in his article 'Working for the Powerdown' (The *Guardian Green Guide*):

'...there is not enough money in the world to offset emissions from flying. Combine all the treasuries and gold reserves and assets and gilt-edged security bonds of every country in the world into one big lump sum and you are still not even close. How much, for example, will it cost to put Bangladesh on stilts? What day-rate were you thinking of paying workers to carry ice and snow to the top of Kilimanjaro?'

Off-setting is just an example of 'green-washing', i.e. corporate propaganda. Companies do not want to move towards becoming carbon neutral, as it affects their profitability. Rather, they 'repackage' their goods and services to appear environmentally friendly.

This book is aimed at trying to help you reduce your emissions towards the goal of zero, within your current situation and means. It's entirely up to you what lifestyle changes you are willing to make and how much time and money you are willing to put into it.

WHY SHOULD I BOTHER?

Save the planet

And not a moment too soon. Our industrial society is producing greenhouse gases, such as carbon dioxide, which trap heat in the earth's atmosphere, which causes global warming, or 'climate change' as it's become known more recently. This in turn is causing glaciers to melt, and extremes of weather conditions such as heat waves, flooding, drought, hurricanes and tornadoes. Many folks still believe that global warming is not scientific fact, that it is still up for debate. If you are one of those who remains unconvinced, then I can recommend no better than to get hold of a copy of Al Gore's film *An Inconvenient Truth*. After watching this fascinating film, you will no longer be in any doubt about this issue.

> Global warming has been talked to death in the media, but still there is doubt amongst the public, a lack of any sense of urgency. Despite the warnings, our race is heading for catastrophe.

We are now in the hottest period of the earth since global temperature records began. The ten hottest years have all been since 1990. The heatwave in Europe in August 2003 caused tens of thousands of deaths, along with a drought which caused a loss of harvests throughout Europe. The debate over whether global warming is real or not is over. Not only is the global temperature at record highs, it is still climbing. The flooding of the south of England in 2007 is just one example of increasingly severe weather conditions which have been linked to global warming.

This is a problem that will not simply go away. And there's worse to come.

Save money!

How would you like to have no bills? This is one of the most pleasant side-effects of leading a completely sustainable life. If you have a sustainable heating system, you will never get a gas bill. Wouldn't that be nice? And with the way fuel prices are going, it's got to be one of the best investments you'll ever make. If you have a £300 annual fuel bill, and it costs £3,000 for a system to be installed, you are earning 10 per cent per year on your investment. As investments go, that's not bad. And as fuel prices go up, so does the amount you are earning.

Most people can appreciate the difference between renting and buying a home. You can live your whole life renting and end up never owning a thing, but buying ensures that, after a number of years, you own your own home. In the same way, by converting one of your bills over to a carbon-neutral alternative, you are simply extending this principle from rent to another of your bills. So instead of 'renting' your heating, you now 'own' your heating. Like buying your own home, it now means that you own the means of production and you'll never have to rent again.

From the humble low-energy bulb to a 50kW wind turbine, the principle remains the same – you are one step closer to being carbon neutral, and one step further away from your bills!

Sustainability

Whatever else you might argue about global warming, our current balance of energy use is completely unsustainable. Every winter in Britain sees fresh headlines about increase in heating bills, petrol prices reach new highs and energy bills go up by 10 to 20 per cent. We are burning fossil fuels for energy at an ever-increasing rate, when the fuels themselves are beginning to decrease in availability.

And yet the energy reaching our planet from the sun in just twenty-four hours is more than all the fossil fuel energy we have ever burned in the history of mankind! We allow this huge resource to go untapped day after day. As fossil fuel depletion sets in hard, there simply won't be a choice – we will have to turn to renewable energy.

Going carbon neutral means becoming sustainable. This also has the added benefit of security of supply. I'm too young to remember the three-day week, when the country was shut down due to striking coal workers, but I'm not too young to remember Ukraine getting its gas supply cut off by Russia. Imagine how invaluable it would be to have a wood stove or geothermal heating in that situation?

Beat the crowds!

Going carbon neutral isn't an 'if', it's a 'when'. Sooner or later every person and every country will be forced to go carbon neutral. When your heating bill is two or three times what it is now, and everyone's switching to wood, or geothermal, or passive solar – do you want to ring up the supplier only to be told there's a two-year waiting list due to demand? The number of people taking up green technologies is increasing every year, but the numbers are still tiny compared to the general population. Now is the perfect time to start.

CONSTRAINTS TO BEING CARBON NEUTRAL

Money

Top of the list. Of all the constraints this has to be the biggest for most people I know. The things we could each do with a million pounds! But this obstacle is not insurmountable, and at the very least we can minimise our impact. Recently, low energy lightbulbs were to be had on offer at my local supermarket for 50p each. Who among us couldn't afford that?

Start small

There are plenty of low budget changes we can all make and these should always be the first. The wind turbine can wait! In fact, the main funding body for renewable projects in Britain, the Low Carbon Buildings Programme, insists that provisions such as insulation and low energy light bulbs already be in place before considering an applicant for funding. After all, what's the point of investing a thousand pounds in a property to generate green electric, if it's being wasted by inefficiency?

As for the larger budget items, there are a couple of options here: borrow or save. Borrowing against your mortgage may be an option, especially in this age of easy finance – but please do your sums! It must be worthwhile and affordable, else you may end up having your carbon neutral house repossessed!

I tend towards the old-fashioned method of saving, since it is secure. In my mind, it adheres to the principle of sustainability. Unless there is any clear reason why buying now rather than later will be of measurable benefit, such as a price increase, I would always save up first, then buy.

Space

What if you live in a flat? Tough call. If you're lacking in space, you can minimise your projects. For example, you could have a small kitchen composter, rather than a full-sized compost bin. You could also go for community projects, rather than householder. For example, growing your own food in a flat wouldn't get you very far, except perhaps a few herbs in the window box. But what about an allotment? It wouldn't be practical to install a wind turbine on a flat, but you could buy in to a cooperative that owns and operates turbines locally, or set one up yourself.

I'd say that this is perhaps one of the most challenging of all situations, but not the end of the world. It means you'll need to think just that little bit further.

Renting

Obviously if you are not a homeowner, then investing money in your property won't offer returns to anyone but the landlord. The most obvious option is to buy your own if you can. Although house prices today are astronomical, there are schemes available which will allow you to buy, say, half of the property, and the other half is then paid for by a Housing Association. If you then later sell the property, you will only recoup half the value. You will still have to weigh up whether it is worth making changes to a property you own only half of, but it is certainly better than renting.

Also, if you rent a council house, the option to buy still exists in most areas once you have been living in the house for a minimum number of years. The price you will be paying may be considerably less than what the property is worth, so is well worth considering.

> If, after considering these options, you are still unable to buy, for whatever reason – you can still make *lifestyle* changes.

Changing lightbulbs for low energy will still benefit you the bill payer, and you can take them with you when you leave. You may also be able to convince the landlord to make changes to the property on the grounds that it will increase the value of the property, and make it more attractive as a rented property. This might include measures such as cavity wall insulation and loft insulation.

If you can't make such significant changes, there are still things you can do. Even though you don't own the property you should be able to get permission to start composting, or to dig a vegetable patch.

Physical ability

Before engaging on any project, consider your physical condition. If you are infirm, then it may not be practical to chop wood for a stove, for example. If any issues such as this do arise, then it may be as well to check what will be required to run any particular appliance or system, ahead of having it installed.

INPUTS AND OUTPUTS

'Enough of the yabbering!' I hear you cry. 'Let's get started!' Ok then, let's get down to the brass tacks of how to go carbon neutral.

The first thing you need to think about is your household, in terms of its inputs and outputs. What does this mean? Think, for example, about heating. Gas central heating might be your input, and losing heat would be your output. So to go carbon neutral you would need to replace your input with a carbon neutral alternative, such as geothermal heating, and insulate your house against heat loss.

Essentially, the input is what you *consume*, be it food, energy or travel. The output is your *waste* products, such as waste food, smoke, or sewage! Once you break down your household into these two categories, the task of handling your carbon emissions becomes much simpler straight away.

The book is broken down into the following sections:

1. Heating

2. Electricity

3. Water

4. Transport

5. Food

6. Shopping.

In each case, the inputs and the outputs will be discussed – what they are, how you probably handle them at the moment, and how you can change them to become carbon neutral. Quite often it is far simpler to change the out-puts than the inputs (with the notable exception of sewage!). So rather than try to solve both the inputs and outputs of one section completely, like food, it is far more rewarding to go through each section in turn and see what you can change straight away, in terms of outputs, without too much head-scratching and wallet-emptying. Far more progress can be made by beginning to compost, than by trying to get a wind turbine installed on your roof!

Take it easy

It is best to tackle these tasks just one at a time. Try not to have too many proj-ects on the go at any one time (something I am guilty of). It can be very demotivating to have a big list of tasks that simply isn't moving. It's far better to have one small task which you can complete in a week or a month.

Start at the bottom. Go for the ones which you might easily accomplish over a weekend first. Take your time before, during and after. Make sure you get adequate quotes for any materials or work you need doing. Also, give your-self and your family time to acclimatise to any changes you make, before moving on to the next one. Just recycling can be a big change to your weekly routine, and if you follow it up with composting as well within a few days, you might end up struggling to keep up your new good habits. You'll start to notice that carbon neutral alternatives often require more physical work and organisation to carry through!

2
Heating

INPUTS

Carbon neutral heating: is it possible? Not only is it possible, but as the years advance, it will become a matter of survival. As we've already mentioned, Britain's oil and gas reserves are depleting fast and the bills are rising even faster. Every time I hear about someone converting from solid fuel to gas, I shake my head in amazement. Gas may be less polluting than coal, but wood is carbon neutral and readily available. Far better to spend the money installing a high efficiency stove or boiler.

Heating primarily refers to heating rooms, but we will also discuss how to heat your hot water supply in this section.

There are five methods of carbon neutral heating:

- wood
- solar hot water
- geothermal heat pump
- passive solar
- electric.

These are in a rough order of feasibility, so we'll start at the bottom and discount those least likely to be implemented.

ELECTRICITY

There is absolutely no reason why a home can't be heated by electricity throughout, and if that electric is drawn from a 100 per cent renewable electric company, or powered by renewable devices such as wind turbines, then the heating system would effectively be carbon neutral.

However, this isn't too practical due to the cost. Having several kilowatt heaters around the home would soon stack up the electric bill! The place for electric heaters will probably be similar to their current role – as a backup to existing heating systems.

Having said this, there is always the option of storage heaters. These are electric heaters which store heat when electricity is available at a cheap rate, usually overnight, then release it throughout the next day. The heat is stored in bricks inside the heater. Obviously, your property needs to be on an electricity tariff which has cheap rate electricity, such as Economy 7.

Using storage heaters

Opinion seems to be deeply divided on the efficiency of storage heaters and the cost of electricity in the UK seems to be escalating at a similar rate to the cost of gas. The main drawbacks of storage heaters are:

- **You must have adequate insulation**. A poorly-insulated property will not be easy to heat with any fuel, but with storage heaters it will soon have you reaching for the peak electric heaters.

- **You need to know how much heat you'll need** *tomorrow*. You'll be setting the controls the night before.

- **You may end up with excess heat**. If the weather turns out milder than expected, it's possible you'll have to open the windows to allow the excess heat to escape.

For some properties, especially isolated rural properties, storage heaters may be a good option. However, do ensure that plenty of capacity is installed.

Using an immersion heater

Without fossil fuels, using a simple immersion heater is probably how most hot water will be supplied. All of the carbon neutral central heating systems available require a separate system for heating hot water, with a few rare exceptions.

Nuclear power stations

As Britain's gas bonanza comes to its end, many of the gas-fired power stations could be supplemented with new nuclear power stations. While it is true that they are carbon neutral, they are controversial and the problem still remains of how to dispose of spent fuel rods. I am making no judgement here about nuclear power, only to point out that any plans for changing your house in Britain should take into account that the electricity market could change radically in the near future, and this may include new nuclear power stations.

PASSIVE SOLAR ENERGY

Passive solar is arguably the cheapest method of heating a home. Once installed it requires *no energy*. Passive solar simply works by having a home that is specially designed to absorb the heat of the sun. The house faces south, and instead of the traditional design of walls, windows and roof, the entire front 'wall' of the house is glass panels which are angled to allow for maximum absorption of the sun. To shade the house in sunny weather, huge blinds are pulled down across the panels. An essential part of such a design is plenty of insulation. The windows are triple-glazed, all doors are draught proof, and the small area of roof, the back wall and floor are all made from insulation material. *And it works*.

A good example of this is the Hockerton Housing Project, north of Nottingham, where four houses have been custom built to exactly this design. They are built in to huge mounds of earth, so that the roof, back and side walls are earth – excellent for insulation. The remainder is large, glass panels and a large conservatory. Each house cost around £95,000 to build, including labour and a wind turbine. However, this was well over 10 years ago, and house prices have changed somewhat since then!

New builds only

The flip side of this, of course, is that it cannot be retro-fitted to an existing home. Some houses already make use of some passive solar, such as conservatories. However, unless you have the means to build a new home from scratch, using passive solar as your sole means of heating isn't an option, and certainly not for a country. Are we about to bulldoze and rebuild Britain's entire housing stock? This is the only reason that passive solar is so low on the list.

GEOTHERMAL HEAT PUMP

If you bore down into the earth, you find that it is warmer than the surface temperature. This is geothermal heat. It is a simple leap of logic then, that water pumped down into the earth will heat itself for free. Pumped back up again, it can then heat a home. The only energy loss here is the electric to power the pump.

Coils of pipes are buried in a trench in the back garden filled with a conducting fluid such as anti-freeze. A heat pump must also be installed, and since these can create some noise and vibration it is best if they are in a utility room or garage, away from the main living area. To take advantage of cheap electricity, these usually run more at night. Finally, an under floor heating system is needed, as most systems do not run hot enough for a radiator system.

How much? According to the Energy Savings Trust, 'A typical 8kW system costs £6,400-£9,600 plus the price of connection to the distribution system. This can vary with property and location'. It appears that this doesn't include the under floor heating system. To offset the cost of installing geothermal heating systems, grants are available from the Low Carbon Buildings Programme of up to £1,200 or 30 per cent of the project, whichever is lower.

For every unit of electricity used to pump the heat, 3–4 units of heat are produced. Initially, this seems appears to make no saving as currently, electricity costs around three times more than gas. However, this ratio will increase over time as gas gradually depletes, and also cheap rate electric at night makes this much more affordable.

Requirements

There are a number of requirements for the system:

- A garden in which to bury the pipes, although in some cases these can be bored vertically. Each system seems to use a different arrangement.
- A well-insulated home, typically a new build.
- Under-floor heating system.

Advantages and disadvantages

The advantages of geothermal heat are obvious: it is an automatic system, without the fuss of having to store and chop wood or rebuild your house, although there will be quite some upheaval, I imagine, during installation.

The main disadvantage is that you will still receive a monthly bill – for the electricity. The difference is that over the years, the equivalent gas bill will gradually increase over the equivalent electric for servicing the system.

The main problem with geothermal heating is that the number of houses suitable for such a system are relatively few. Not only does the house need to have a garden for burying the coils, it needs to have the under-floor heating system pre-installed, and the house itself needs to be a new-build with certain layers of insulating foam built into the walls inside and out. This is a tall order, and applies to a very small percentage of current housing stock. Fitting such a system to an older house would simply exchange a high gas bill for a high electricity bill.

Although at present there are very few of these systems installed in Britain each year, this could soon rise as fuel bills climb yet higher. In Sweden, the expense of fitting geothermal heating systems is even higher than Britain, but far more many systems are sold each year. Why? Because of the scarcity and expense of fossil fuels there. As this situation begins to appear in Britain, it is likely that those who are able will begin to take after the Swedes.

SOLAR HOT WATER

This has to be the most overlooked carbon neutral heating system available. These systems are as efficient as they're probably ever going to be. They can be fitted to an existing system with little fuss in a short period of time. They are perfect for running alongside your existing hot water system, such as gas or the immersion heater. And as long as the sun is shining, you have a tank full of hot water for free. According to the LCBP, they 'can provide almost all of your hot water during the summer months and about 50 per cent year round'.

These should be fitted to all 'new build' homes by law, in my opinion. Of course there is an initial setup cost, as with all systems. However, this should pay itself back within ten years, probably five, depending on your usage.

The system works regardless of the ambient temperature, so a sunny winter's day will provide the same hot water as a sunny summer's day. But even on a cloudy day, it's not unusual to achieve temperatures of 20° in the water tank. This can then be topped up with the immersion heater for a bath.

Types of solar delivery system

There are two types of delivery system – direct and indirect.

The **direct heating system** works by having a solar panel, which heats up a small chamber of water on the roof. Once it is a number of degrees hotter than the hot water tank, a pump will switch on. This pumps the heated water down from the chamber to the tank, and in turn pumps cooler water back up to the chamber. Then the whole process begins again.

The **indirect delivery system** works by having an intermediary liquid, which is pumped up to the roof. This heating fluid is heated in a similar way, and then is pumped back down to a heat exchanger, which then heats the hot water tank.

The two delivery systems are similar, but the direct system tends to be cheaper, as there is no need for a heat exchanger. However there may be some heat loss in the colder months; if you are pumping water up to the roof, the pipes may freeze and burst on a cold night. To prevent this, hot water is pumped from the tank back up to the roof, essentially the reverse of the heating process. Heat loss does tend to be minimal. In indirect systems, the heating fluid which is exposed on the roof, freezes at temperatures far below zero, so there is no chance of burst pipes in this case.

Types of solar panel

There are two types of panel – flat plate and evacuated tube.

The **flat plate** system is less efficient, but cheaper to install. It essentially uses flat plates of darkened metal to absorb sunlight and transmit the heat. The **evacuated tube** system uses vacuum-sealed glass tubes, with a slender channel of heat-conducting fluid at the centre which carries the heat up to the pipe at the top. Evacuated tubes are the more efficient system, however they have a reputation for losing their seal after a time, as the tube heats and cools over the years.

Summing up

These systems are a perfect accompaniment to the other central heating systems on the list, and immediately resolve the issue of having to run a wood-fired system on a hot summer's day just to heat up the water.

The costs involved can vary from as little as £2,000 to as much as £5,000, so shop around and see what you can find. When looking at buying a system, don't just look at cost, but also at efficiency and any potential issues such as the water pump breaking down, or water leakage. If possible, try to get to see a working system when the sun is shining, so you can see what temperatures you will get.

The Low Carbon Buildings Programme funds solar hot water systems for £400 up to a maximum of 30 per cent of the project.

Wood

When wood is burned it creates heat and smoke – carbon. That smoke is then absorbed back into a tree, and so the cycle carbon neutral is complete. Tried and tested for thousands of years, it is simple and practical. And as technology marches on we have ever more efficient wood burners – so efficient in fact, that they are suitable for burning in a smoke control zone. This efficiency is obtained by moving the flow of smoke so that it is burned over and over, until all useful energy has been taken from it, leaving only a tiny whisp of smoke. Many are billed as being 70 per cent efficient, as opposed to an open fire which is around 30 per cent efficient.

Smoke control areas

There are several models of wood burner that are exempt from the smoke control regulations, due to their high efficiency and low emissions. The full list for the UK is here: http://www.uksmokecontrolareas.co.uk/appliances. php?country=e

Types of wood burners

Wood-fuelled burners come in all shapes and sizes, but break down into boilers and stoves. Most of the appliances which are approved for funding by the LCBP or by the smoke control authorities only use wood pellets as their fuel, which have to be ordered. The reason for the move towards pellet burners is that they are easier to automate. A hopper (feed mechanism) on the top of a boiler or stove can be filled and the appliance itself will take in pellets as required. It doesn't need to be constantly tended like a log stove, for example.

Grants and funding

The LCBP provides grants for approved appliances on the following basis:

1. Room heater/stoves automated wood pellet feed: overall maximum of £600 or 20 per cent of the relevant eligible costs, whichever is the lower;

2. Wood-fuelled boiler systems: overall maximum of £1,500 or 30 per cent of the relevant eligible costs, whichever is the lower.

The full list of approved appliances for LCBP funding are available here: http://www.clear-skies.org/households/RecognisedProducts.aspx

Boiler or stove?

Boilers can be transplanted into existing central heating systems, simply substituting a wood boiler for existing gas or oil boilers. Access and fuelling have to be considered here, depending on the make and model of boiler to be fitted. They are not designed to be a centrepiece for your hearth, but a functional piece of kit to be hidden away at the back of your house, like a gas boiler.

Stoves on the other hand directly heat a single room, and can be pleasant to view. However, when it comes to pellet stoves, this means that each room will require its own stove with ventilation and fuelling issues.

The happy medium you may wish to consider is an efficient wood stove (as opposed to a pellet stove), *with a back boiler*. These can burn dry wood and heat the hot water tank, and central heating system. There are also several which are approved for use in a smoke control zone (for example the British-made Yorkshire Stove from Dunsley). The only drawback here is that the LCBP has not approved a single wood stove for funding, so you will have to find the full amount yourself.

Points to consider

The discrepancies between the LCBP and the smoke control regulations can be quite frustrating. Most of the appliances approved for funding for wood or pellet burning are *not* approved for a smoke control zone. Given that the objective here is to move towards becoming carbon neutral and to avoid pollution, this seems puzzling to say the least. So take plenty of time when considering how to convert your system over to carbon neutral, thinking about:

- **Type of appliance**: boiler or stove.

- **Type of fuel**: logs, wood, pellets or other, such as switchgrass. This will be determined by the appliance, but you ought to have some idea of the fuel you'll be sourcing, and its cost.

- **Funding required**: together with the two items above, this will restrict your choice of system. If you are willing to forgo funding, then this will widen your choice. But if you will need the funding to complete the job, then look carefully at which systems you can choose.

- **Smoke control zone**: as mentioned above, surprisingly few appliances are on both the LCBP and smoke control approved lists, so check this list also if you are siting an appliance in a smoke control zone.

- **Your house**: do you have a chimney? Many houses nowadays are built for gas, without a chimney. You will have to speak to your installer about this.

- **Wood source**: do investigate where the wood is sourced from. If your supplier is deforesting areas of natural beauty, then you may as well stick to gas! Ideally waste or recycled wood should be burned where possible, or at least wood from sustainable, local sources.

Advantages and disadvantages

There are several drawbacks to having a wood-fuelled heating system.

- **Cost of fitting**: The cost of having a gas central heating system refitted for wood is around £5,000 at time of writing. If you are wary of switching your whole system over, it is possible to have a dual-fuel home – wood and gas. Of course, such a system would cost more. Ask your local heating engineer for quotes. Bear in mind that even your *installer* must be on the approved list for funding, not just the appliance. So if funding is an issue, ensure you go with an approved installer.
- **Supply of fuel**: It must somehow be sourced. This isn't usually too difficult – we get all our wood for free from a local workshop. It's amazing how much wood folks actually throw out. If you can get the word out that you're after wood, you will probably get it coming to your front door. (Of course, wood must also be stored somewhere dry such as a wood shed, and possibly chopped up if it isn't available in smaller pieces.)
- **The system is manual**: You have to fuel the fire, and clean out the ash. This is the part that many people dread, having ash all over their living room. But it needn't be the case – metal ash carriers of all sizes are available for around £40 from specialists 'Tippy', among others.
- **Hot water in the summer**: Some people burn their fire all year round; most efficient boilers can heat enough water for a bath in as little as twenty minutes. But it may be as well to use the immersion instead. Who wants a roaring fire in the height of summer? The perfect complement to the wood-fuelled system is the hot water solar panel, heating the water throughout the summer months.

But despite these drawbacks, a wood-fuelled heating system may still be the best option for many. Despite the need for sourcing fuel, it is often free or very cheap. This alone should offset the cost of the initial system within ten years at the most. With the efficiency of systems improving all the time, the amount of wood consumed is far less than an open fire. And it is also reliable. Even if the pump breaks down, you can still heat at least one room in the house. That has a lot to be said for it.

Heating requirements

When it comes to selecting an appliance, you will need to buy one that is adequate for your heating needs. Heating systems are measured in BTUs (British Thermal Units), e.g. 40,000 BTUs. To calculate roughly the BTUs of the property you are heating, you will need about 5.95 BTUs per cubic foot (0.02 cubic metres) of room space (down to about 5.45 with double glazing and good insulation). But this is only a rough estimate, and a heating engineer will be able to give you a more accurate figure. You also need to remember to include an extra 10,000 BTUs for the hot water.

OUTPUTS

The issue here is *insulation*. Before spending thousands on a new heating system, you would be as well to consider spending just a few hundred insulating your home. Ironically, when it comes to insulation, the cheapest measures are often the most efficient. Double glazing, which costs several thousand pounds, only reaps a saving of around £20-30 per year, with a payback period of around 100 years! At the other end of the scale, a cylinder jacket will cost around £10 and pay itself back in less than twelve months. So don't splash out on expensive systems straight away; get the basics right first.

INSULATING YOUR HOME

Our homes lose heat from all points of contact with the outside. This includes:

- walls 35%
- floors 15%
- roof 25%
- doors 15%
- windows 10%.

Every box needs to be ticked to save heat, energy and money. The good news is that this is probably the cheapest, most cost effective improvement you can make to your home. Government funding is available to *everyone* and low income groups may receive many of these benefits for free. (Please note that costs were correct at the time of writing.)

Loft insulation: this should be 25 cm thick. £100 (fitted) from the local city council, free for many. Saving of £50 per year.

Cavity wall insulation: £125 from the council, return of £80 per year.

Cylinder jacket: £10 from a DIY shop, saving of £15 per year.

Extra thick curtains: cost and return will vary here. You don't need to replace existing curtains, simply purchase a liner that hangs alongside on the same set of curtain hooks. You might also consider putting up a curtain across front and back doors for extra insulation.

Draught excluders: these vary from the DIY variety for old socks, to fitted rubber seals around doors.

Radiator reflectors: £7.50 each, save £5–15 per year. Anywhere up to 40 per cent of the heat from a radiator on an outside wall can be lost immediately. Straightforward reflectors return that heat back to the room.

Other options are available, but they are costly and take many years to pay themselves back. They include:

High efficiency boilers: condensing boilers, combi-boilers, etc. They operate on the premise of efficiency. They also operate on gas. I'd be much happier spending this money on switching to a wood boiler or geothermal heating.

Insulating wallpaper: very expensive and time consuming for what it returns, but in a perfect world every house would be papered in it.

Double glazing: bottom of the list. Expensive and returns very little. Also expensive to maintain, as breakages and replacements require a replacement unit, rather than just glass. That unit is made with plastic, and plastic is made from oil. Over the coming years we may return to simple wood and glass.

If you are unsure about how to set about getting your home insulated, then pick up the phone and call one of the many agencies out there that have been set up to help. The Energy Savings Trust (www.est.org) would be a good place to start. In many areas there are schemes running to help people insulate their home, many for free or at a substantial discount. More than any other step, insulation will probably be the biggest contribution you make to reducing carbon emissions. So what are you waiting for?

3

Electricity

INPUTS

Generating electricity from renewable sources seems to be a flagship for the carbon neutral movement. Everyone knows what a wind turbine is, or a solar panel. But very rarely do we ever see them in practice, and not without reason. Every step of installing such an item can cause problems. It can be a major issue just getting to grips with the terminology, so let's take it one step at a time.

Types of system

There are two *types* of electrical system for connecting generators to your home – the **standalone** system, whereby *all* your electricity comes from your devices, and the **grid-connected** system whereby you are still connected to the grid, but you only draw *some* of your electricity from the device.

THE STANDALONE SYSTEM

The standalone system is suitable for a remote farm, for example, where the cost of being connected to the grid is so high that it would be a similar cost to set up your own generation system. The issue here is what happens when there isn't enough supply from the devices, such as calm days for a wind turbine. Typically, this is taken care of via a bank of batteries which can both store extra energy on days when there is a surplus, or provide a backup on slack days.

However, a battery system is high on maintenance, and can be a messy business. It will also wear down over time and need replacing. It does seem that more advanced batteries are on the horizon, but we'll have to see how they pan out.

As you can see from Figure 1, the main components of a standalone system are:

- **Batteries and charge regulator**: connected to the generation devices, the batteries are responsible for storing electricity, and supplying current as required. The charge regulators prevent the batteries from being overcharged, and dump excess current.

- **Low voltage disconnects**: these prevent too low a current being supplied from the batteries as they discharge.

- **Inverter**: converts DC current into AC for supply to 240V appliances.

- **Distribution box**: distribution of current including fuses and circuit breaker.

Obviously, there is more to such a system than simply the renewable devices themselves, and this should be taken into consideration. If you are fortunate enough to have a source of running water on your property, you could consider hydro-electricity. These systems have the advantage of being a fairly consistent flow, especially with a small reservoir (such as an old mill pond). Batteries for such an installation becomes much less of an issue if the flow is sufficiently consistent.

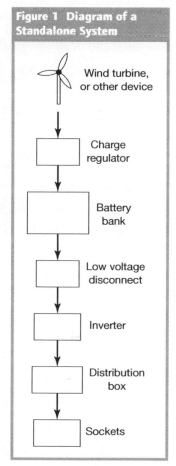

Figure 1 Diagram of a Standalone System

Wind turbine, or other device

Charge regulator

Battery bank

Low voltage disconnect

Inverter

Distribution box

Sockets

THE GRID-CONNECTED SYSTEM

A grid-connected system utilises the grid instead of a battery bank for surpluses and shortfalls; buying or selling electricity from and to the grid as needs be. But let's clear up a myth here straight away – if the grid goes down, so does your electricity. Just because you have a grid-connected device such as a wind turbine, it doesn't make you immune to blackouts. Whenever the network operator needs to take down an area of the grid, they will shut down all devices inputting to the grid. This is to make that area safe for engineers.

Permission must be gained from the grid supplier for the connection of any new devices to the grid, and there are certain technical requirements as well as a meter and contract.

- Permission from your local Distribution Network Operator (DNO). This involves making sure that you have a properly approved invertor which will shut off on demand.

- Buy-back agreement: An agreement must be reached with a power supplier as to how power will be supplied and bought back, specifically at what price. Not all power companies do them for small devices (i.e. less than 50kW). Good Energy is one company that will consider smaller appliances.

- Two-way meter: a meter needs to be fitted which measures electricity into and out of the property. (Note that this will depend on how you are planning to sell the electricity generated.)

As you can see from Figure 2, the grid-connected system is simplified. Elements such as the inverter and distribution box are still present, but without the necessity of a battery bank and all it entails. Also, there is no need to depart from the security of the grid if your devices should break down or be in need of maintenance, for example. With a battery-powered system, you are entirely dependent on the storage capacity of the batteries.

Figure 2 Diagram of a Grid-Connected System

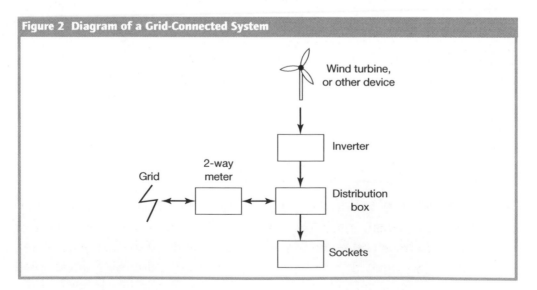

Types of device

The choice of renewable energy devices for a householder has exploded in the last few years. They now include the following:

- wind turbine

- solar electricity (photovoltaic/PV)

- hydro electricity

- combined heat & power (CHP).

WIND TURBINE

Not so long ago, wind turbines were impossible to install near residences, let alone attached to them. Now there are a range of devices running up to 1.5kW which can be installed for a reasonable price on a residential property, and increasingly planning departments are looking favourably upon such installations. Turbines in the UK suitable for installation on a property include the Eclectic Stealthgen, Renewable Devices' Swift and Windsave's WS1000. (It should also be borne in mind, however, that although Britain has the largest wind reserves in Europe, there will still be areas where there is insufficient wind to support a turbine, regardless of size.)

Objections

There is, unfortunately, a strong element of NIMBYism (Not In My Back Yard) in the UK, fuelled by ignorance. Bizarre but common objections include that turbines distract drivers, panic horses, kill birds, damage the environment and cause epileptic fits! Denmark has half the world market share of wind turbines. Why their streets aren't full of wrecked cars, dead birds and people having fits is a mystery. This knee-jerk reaction is likely to be the largest obstacle to erecting a turbine on your home.

Reasonable objections in the past have included noise and vibration, but with the advent of ultra-quiet turbines, these objections on the grounds of noise can be safely overturned. Nowadays, the noise of such an urban turbine is likely to be drowned out by the sound of rustling leaves from a nearby tree.

This doesn't mean that your neighbours' objections to any planned activity can be ignored. In fact, objections should be carefully documented and responded to. However, you should be aware that in addition to quite reasonable objections, you are also likely to be greeted by a parade of paranoid fantasies!

Solar electricity (Photovoltaic/PV)

Electric solar panels, otherwise known as photovoltaic (PV) panels, are iconic. As a clean, quiet source of electricity, they seem to safely avoid the wrath that turbines attract. They require no planning permission to speak of, and can be hooked into domestic electricity the same as any other renewable device.

So why don't we see more PV panels? It really comes down to their expense and inefficiency. As we'll see shortly, when considering a renewable device the cost per kW provided needs to be examined. PV panels can easily cost twice that of a turbine. The other issue in the UK is, of course, the lack of sunshine! Although this isn't necessarily an issue with an efficient device (such as solar hot water), it can produce disappointing results with PV panels.

In places such as California, where the sun is constant and the electricity expensive, it can make good sense to have a PV system rather than a turbine. However, in the UK, which has tremendous wind reserves across most of the country, electricity from turbines will always be cheaper kW for kW. Having said this, PV panels are highly funded, to the tune of £2,000 per kWp (kilowatt peak). See 'Grants available' on page 48 for further details.

Of course, solar electricity is easier to maintain as it has no moving parts. Larger turbines need to have the bearings greased each year, for example. Not so with a solar panel. So although solar electricity may not be a first choice, it should certainly not be ruled out for home installation. A common solution is to use a turbine as the primary device, then PV panels as a backup.

Hydro electricity

Hydro electricity is as near perfect as you can get for renewable energy, provided you have plenty of land and a flow of water across it. Unfortunately, that rules most of us out. If you *are* lucky enough to be in this position, then do capitalise on it. It hasn't been investigated in the UK in any great depth, and the outlay for such a system can be substantial, but it is likely to provide all your electricity with spare to sell. Like wind turbines it requires planning permission, but attracts little or no prejudice.

It is difficult to provide specific advice here regarding the installation of such a system, as each one will be different. There are some companies specialising in this type of device and the internet is the best place to seek them out. Hydro has the advantage of a smooth, predictable supply of electric providing the flow of water keeps up, and by building a reservoir, no matter how small, this regularity can be enhanced. This was the principle of the mill pond.

However, the closest any of us is likely to get to such a system is in a community project.

COMBINED HEAT AND POWER (CHP)

Combined Heat and Power is essentially a boiler and an electricity generator rolled into one. And although it sounds like a magic bullet for home heat and energy generation, it is more like a pipe dream at the moment. The technology is still far too immature for domestic installation and is mainly found in industry, if at all.

One of the biggest drawbacks is that the few units which have been on offer for domestic users run on gas. This is obviously not carbon neutral, and really just gives home users the option of running their own mini-power station. Ideally, of course, the fuel would be wood, or some other carbon neutral alternative. Unfortunately, this option is still a long way off.

> Another big problem with many CHP units is the noise. Many are essentially engines, and consequently they are extremely noisy – a bit like starting up a motorbike in your kitchen!

This is a hangover from their industrial origins, and they are often to be found powering factories and the like.

Research has been moving forward in this area, and one such offering in recent years has been the Whispergen from Powergen. These are reputed to be much quieter (hence the name) and are especially designed for the domestic consumer. As at the time of writing, however, the Whispergen was not on the market, although information can be found on www.powergen.co.uk

Another drawback of such units is that often they offer heat and electricity *at the same time*, not separately. This could be tremendously wasteful. Who wants heat during the summer? When you consider the issue of depletion, any new appliances using gas really are redundant. Of course, CHP units fuelled by wood or biomass may be just around the corner, but at present if you want to install a CHP unit in your home, the pickings are rather slim.

The main bonus with generating electricity with a CHP unit is that the supply of energy provided is smooth and predictable. Wind turbines and solar panels are anything but, hence the need for battery backup or grid-connection.

Funding is currently being considered by the LCBP, even for CHP units which run on gas and other fossil fuels such as LNG, so if you have got your heart set on such a device it may be worth holding off for a few years to allow this area to develop and be recognised.

INSTALLING A SYSTEM

How do I go about getting one of these systems?

1. Make efficiency savings in your home (do *not* skip this).

2. Decide how much electricity (kWh) you'll need.

3. Select system type (standalone or grid-connected).

4. Choose types of devices (e.g. solar panel, hydro electric, etc.).

5. Select your makes and models.

   ▨ Calculate kWh provided by chosen devices compared to total from step 2.

   ▨ Will this appliance attract a grant?

   ▨ Get quotes for purchase and installation.

6. Engage an electrician.

7. Make legal agreements.

   ▨ Permission for grid connection with the DNO.

   ▨ Buy-back agreement with power company.

8. Apply for planning permission.

9. Apply for grants.

10. Install your system.

This whole list probably looks quite daunting at first glance, but as a friend of mine used to say, 'Nothing at all in the world is complicated, it's just a lot of simple things added together.' And he was right. Each of these steps is pretty straightforward. Even applying for planning permission can itself be broken down into a number of simple steps. So let's look at each step in detail.

1. Make efficiency savings in your home

For *how* to make your home more efficient, see 'Outputs', later in this section. This step should not be skipped! It can make a huge difference to how much you will have to pay out for devices. The homes at the Hockerton Housing Project, for example, use only half the amount of electricity of the average home. This means they only need devices to generate half the power. And when devices cost in the thousands, this is something you're going to want to do!

The LCBP *will not consider an application for a grant* if the home involved does not have efficiency measures already implemented. The LCBP website states:

> 'You must undertake a number of energy efficiency measures before you are eligible to apply for a low carbon buildings grant. These measures will ensure that you are minimising your energy requirements. Before applying we require you to have:
>
> a. insulated the whole of the loft of the property to meet current building regulations e.g. 270mm of mineral wool loft insulation or suitable alternative
> b. installed cavity wall insulation (if you have cavity walls)
> c. fitted low energy light bulbs in all appropriate light fittings
> d. installed basic controls for your heating system to include a room thermostat and a programmer or timer.'

So even if you're not bothered about being efficient, any grant you are applying for is dependent on these measures being taken.

A good device you may want to invest in is the Plug-In Mains Power & Energy Monitor. Not only does it tell you the current drawn by a device, but you can leave it plugged in to get the total kWh used over a month or so. Extremely useful if you're not sure of a device's exact load. These are available from several outlets for £15 or less at the time of writing. Also very useful in the next step…

2. Decide how much electricity (kWh) you'll need

Ok, so how much? Well, the average home in the UK uses about 2.5kW. This is highest in the evening, and lowest at night. The simplest way to measure how much you're going to need is to look at your current bill. This should tell you how many kWh (one kW for one hour) you use on a regular basis.

You might see a line like this:

Price (kWh@p)

99@3.199

In this example, you have used 99 kWh for this type of electricity, at 3.199p per kWh. Add up the number of kWh you have used, and divide it by the number of days for the period covered by your bill, to get the average kWh used per day. You can multiply this by 365 to get the number of kWh you will use in a year. If you haven't implemented efficiency measures yet, make these and then re-examine your bill.

If you don't have a bill to examine, for example if you are moving into a new property, then you'll need to go around the whole property and look at each device in turn, measure its rating and multiply this by the number of hours it will be in use each day (on average). Not all systems will be rated, such as the pump for your central heating system for example, but try to be as accurate as possible. (The Plug-In Energy Monitor might come in handy again here.)

Also, if you are buying a new house, the newly-launched Home Information Packs (HIPs) should be helpful. Each one has to include an Energy Performance Certificate. This will give the property an Energy Efficiency Rating from A–G (A is the most, and G the least, efficient). Incidentally, it also includes the property's Environmental Impact Rating from A–G as well, in terms of carbon dioxide emissions.

Remember that although you may be using far more than 2.5kW at any point in time (just the vacuum cleaner might be 2kW, for example), you are looking at an average spaced out over a year. The spacing out is done either by batteries (for a standalone system) or by the national grid (for a grid-connected system), enabling you to draw extra current when needed or save it for later if not.

The figure you want to have in front of you by the end of this step is a number of kWh per year. If at all possible, have some leeway built in, espe-cially if you are going to be relying on a battery bank. Of course, if you are grid-connected, then you don't initially need to worry about replacing your *whole* energy requirement, you can draw some from devices and continue to draw the rest from the grid.

3. Select system type

Standalone (with battery backup) or grid-connected? This will depend on your circumstances and will determine how the rest of the system is laid out. You may have to revisit this step when it comes to costing.

4. Choose types of devices

You've probably already made this decision, or at least have a good idea. You may have your heart set on a wind turbine, or solar panels. These two are your most likely choice for homes in the UK, a combination of the two helping smooth the input over the year.

You also want to be quite clear at this stage where the devices are going to be installed. For example, if you are looking at PV panels, then look at your roof and consider how close to south-facing it is. This can affect your funding as well as the amount of electricity you will draw in. When considering a wind turbine, think if it is going to be mounted on the side of your house (for semi or detached), or be free standing. How easy will it be to get to for maintenance or repair?

To get the full installation requirements it is a good idea to contact a potential manufacturer or fitter.

5. Select your makes and models

At this stage, you really are ready to look around at specific wind turbines, solar panels, etc. The main issues here are **power** and **price**.

Checking the price

It's unlikely you need me to tell you to check the price of these units first, but when it comes to buying electrical generation devices, the price you want to look at is *price per kW*. This is similar to looking at two brands of cereal, for example, and comparing the price per kilo. Sadly, most companies don't advertise the price, only their devices, so you'll have to ring up directly and ask for a quote. Quite surprisingly, companies selling renewable energy devices seem to be quite relaxed about their sales. Often, they will take their device off the market for twelve months at a time for various reasons. An e-mail or phone enquiry can take weeks to yield results, so be prepared to take some time and to have to chase up enquiries. At this stage, an estimate is enough to get you started.

Checking the power

Is there going to be enough power to cover the usage of your property? This is a tricky question, and one you may only be able to estimate. Wind and solar are rated at a standard amount of input – for example wind turbines are rated at a number of kW generated when the wind speed is 12 metres per second, whereas the wind speed will vary throughout the year. Solar panels are rated in kWp (kilowatt peak). This is the number of kilowatts generated when the solar panel is at its peak amount of sunshine.

Wind turbines often return from 1,000-2,000 hours per year at their rated power. So a 0.5kW turbine is likely to give you from 500-1,000 kWh per year. For a good estimate of what wind speeds you can expect in your area, visit:

www.dti.gov.uk/energy/sources/renewables/renewables-explained/wind-energy/page27326.html

This includes useful information for calculating your average wind speed. But also use your common sense. If your house or area is very sheltered, then don't expect high wind speeds regardless of what is indicated by the wind speed database. Ideally, contact someone nearby who already has a similar device fitted and ask how much electricity they get in a year.

> Whether the power generated throughout the year from a renewable device is enough to cover your household demand is going to be more of an issue if you are planning on a standalone system than if you are going for grid-connected.

Devices eligible for a grant

The next thing to consider when selecting a specific brand of renewable device is, if it is on the approved list of appliances for a grant. Do not assume that just because you are buying a solar panel, for example, it is funded. The LCBP only approves a grant for specific appliances. The full list is available at: http://www.clear-skies.org/ households/RecognisedProducts.aspx

Factors to consider

To begin selecting the appropriate make and model of device, make a list of each of the companies, and each of their devices, in a grid. Use the following columns for comparison:

1. Company

2. Device name

3. Power rating

4. Price for device (inc. VAT)

5. Price for installation, including all wiring devices (inc. VAT)

6. Funding which can be recouped from grants

7. Total cost per kW

8. Date last contacted.

Remember that a small turbine's minimum speed should be between 2.5 – 5m/s before it starts generating electricity. This is because at low kW ratings, you need to take full advantage of the range of wind speeds available, especially for a rooftop device.

You may also want to ask about annual maintenance. In most cases this is negligible for small turbines. But for those rated 5kW+, it may be necessary to grease the bearings once a year. This will mean the turbine has to be taken down somehow. Getting a quote for this annual event may save you much aggravation further down the line.

All other things being equal, the company you are looking for is the one with the *lowest cost per kW*. This should include all costs, including installation.

Installation

In each case, the installation process will be different. Some companies offer you the device and nothing more, others will insist on doing the full installation themselves. In each case, you need a total cost for the device, including installation, then divide it by the power rating to get the cost per kW. You may need to go to an electrician for a quote for the installation, if this isn't covered by the company selling the renewable energy device.

Also, bear in mind that if you are looking at a combination of devices, such as wind turbine and solar panels, their installation together must be harmonious. If you have two companies, who both insist on installing the full system, there could be problems, and you might end up paying for two lots of installation!

Another snag here to be careful of is that to qualify for a grant, not only must the appliance be approved, but also the *installer*. Having said this, it's not too difficult to get an approved installer, but check 'Useful Information' to make sure they are on the list.

Rooftop turbines

It can't have escaped many people's notice that rooftop turbines have received something of a battering in the press. One suggestion is that the turbines are performing significantly less successfully than the manufacturers claim.

The gist of the argument seems to be that wind turbines need to be clear of obstacles such as trees and rooftops to function at full capacity, and since home turbines are, by their very nature, close to buildings, they are unlikely to get their full yield.

No one seems to be contesting that there will be a reduction in performance the question is how much of a reduction. Sadly, there seem to be no hard figures coming from either side of the argument, just anonymously quoted consultants.

So until we can get some figures for micro-turbines on our rooftops, we'll just have to take our chances. But when our turbine goes up, I'll be glad to publish my monthly figures on the internet!

6. Engage an electrician

For this stage you will need the help of a qualified electrician. The company selling you the generation device may be willing to help out in this respect. The object of the exercise here, is to draw out on paper how the system will operate, a circuit diagram of sorts. At one end you should have your generation devices, and at the other, your household appliances. What you need to know is how the electricity is going to get from one end to the other.

It may also be necessary to revisit this step once you have decided on your devices, as some have an inverter or other device installed within the unit. Also, some companies installing generation devices will want to do this part themselves.

Typically a system will require the following wiring devices:

Standalone

- renewable appliances (e.g. wind turbine)

- charge regulator (one for each appliance)

- battery bank

- low voltage disconnect

- inverter

- fuse box and distribution

Grid-connected

- renewable appliances

- inverter

- fuse box and distribution

- two-way meter.

With the help of your electrician, a circuit diagram can be mapped out, and the items required can be selected. At this stage, a quote for the electrical installation can be obtained, including the cost for any items which will need to be bought. The electrician or company making the installation should be the ones selecting the items required (e.g. inverter).

It is essential that any appliances (especially the inverter) are G83/1 compliant. This is the regulation that governs whether an item can be connected to the grid or not (see next section).

7. Make legal agreements

Primarily, this step is for those who will be setting up a grid-connected system. Those running a standalone system can ignore this. There are a few flaming hoops to jump through here.

DNO approval

Your Distribution Network Operator (DNO) is responsible for running your area of the grid. A full list of DNOs can be found from the Energy Networks Association by visiting http://www.energynetworks.org or by calling 020 7706 5100.

You will need to get your DNO's permission to connect any devices to the grid. Essentially this is covered by a document called the G83/1, which was drawn up as a recommendation by the Energy Networks Association. However, although it began life as a recommendation it is now *mandatory* to comply with this standard. Your DNO should explain what you need to know when you speak to them.

For a small domestic installation such as the home turbines we are discussing here, you simply need to fill in a form and let your DNO know what is going on. As long as all your equipment is G83/1 compliant, then nothing should be amiss. Ensuring that your equipment is compliant is something that your installer should take care of.

However, if you are planning to install a much bigger generator, such as a community turbine, then a formal application will need to be made, with full details of your proposal in partnership with your installer. The dividing line given by our area DNO when we enquired was anything up to 16 amps (for the technically aware), but obviously this should be checked out directly with your DNO upon application.

Buy-back agreement

If you're grid-connected you can sell back any excess electricity to the grid. When I first heard this I thought that as I would only be generating a small amount, there wouldn't be any to sell back. But with renewable generation technologies, although your *annual* production may not exceed your usage, because the supply is irregular you'll often have an excess at odd times. Wind turbines produce a lot of energy at night, for example, but most of your requirement will be during the day or evening.

Selling excess electricity can only be done through your power company. Unfortunately, many power companies are not interested in buying back small amounts of electricity, which to you and me is anything below a megawatt! So you might have to switch power company. A couple of companies which *do* enter into buy-back agreements with micro-generators such as you are Green Energy and Good Energy (see Useful Information – Green Power Companies). Physically, you'll need to install a two-way meter, instead of the standard one-way meter, for billing. Again, this is something that your installer should take care of.

> The main way of buying and selling electricity is that you have to buy at retail rates, but sell at wholesale, so obviously there is going to be a disparity in the prices.

However, the number of different tariffs available seems to have exploded of late, and now some companies will pay you for *every* kWh generated, but at a lower rate. Like shopping around for retail electricity, you may want to try several tariffs before settling on the one which seems to pay the most.

Renewable Obligation Certificate

The Renewable Obligation was brought in to ensure that power generators produce a minimum percentage of their electricity from renewable sources. Each generator of renewable electricity gets a Renewable Obligations Certificate (ROC) per MWh per year to show this. These are issued by Ofgem. So what?

Well, if a generator hasn't got enough ROCs to cover their obligation, then they have to pay into a fund which is then divided up between those who have got ROCs. A micro-turbine (for example) is worth about one ROC. At the time of writing, one ROC was worth about £60. So, basically, you can get paid to produce green electricity. However, there is a certain amount of red tape before you get paid. To find out exactly what steps to take, you need to contact Ofgem (www.ofgem.gov.uk).

8. Apply for planning permission

After wading through items one to seven above, it will come as unwelcome news that this may be your biggest step! It is not unusual to have to resubmit planning applications, and make appeals to get a wind turbine approved, even one as small as a rooftop domestic turbine. Solar panels and CHP units usually do not require planning permission, and hydro-electric generators are unique. For this section then, it is assumed we are applying for planning permission for a wind turbine. For other systems, skip to the next step.

Elevation diagram

In order to apply for planning permission for anything, a detailed plan must be included. The most suitable for a wind turbine is an elevation. When preparing plans for submission, ensure that they are drawn exactly as specified by your guidance notes. This includes using the correct materials, scale and units, and may vary between councils.

If you phone up an architect for a quote for this you will probably get a price of around £1,000. If this was the only option, it would double the cost for a Windsave turbine! It seems pedantic to ask for a diagram of a wind turbine installation when no permission is required for a satellite dish, but the law is the law. Fortunately, there are other options. The first is to look in the small ads of your local paper for a plan drawer. These are folks who will simply measure up and draw you a diagram cheaply, probably for a few hundred pounds. The other option is to draw it yourself.

Doing it yourself

When I first began this, I was lucky enough to speak to a very friendly architect. When I explained the situation, he suggested I draw the diagram myself. 'But how can I measure the height of my house without surveying equipment? Or my roof?' I asked. He responded by saying that the best way to get measurements suitable for such a diagram is *to count bricks*. Get yourself a sheet of graph paper and go for a scale of 1cm to 1m. Then go outside and measure the length of 5 bricks and the height of 10 bricks. By counting the number of bricks along each height and length of your house, you should then be able to calculate the dimensions for your diagram.

If you have any awkward measurements, such as a sloping roof, you will need to get a good distance away, and possibly gain height, and take a photo of your property. You may have to ask a neighbour across the road if you can take a photo from their upstairs window!

Once the photo is developed, you can measure your dimensions with a ruler. If you have a dimension you already know (from counting and measuring bricks), you can measure this on the photo with a ruler. The photo then becomes your scale diagram. If the width of your house is 5m and on the photo it is 5cm, then you can measure other lines which are unknown and calculate their lengths.

Turbine dimensions

The next stage in this process is to add a scale image of your proposed turbine to the scale diagram of your house, where it will be sited. It may be on a pole up the side of your house, or on a bracket mounting. You will need to get exact dimensions of the various parts of the turbine, so that you can give the planning officers an idea of how the turbine will look, and how it will impact on your neighbours and the surrounding area.

Ideally, you will be provided with such a diagram, to the scale of 1:100, by your turbine suppliers, which you can then trace directly onto your diagram. If this has not been supplied in advance, then you will need to contact your turbine supplier and ask for it. As this is a new industry, the companies involved are still finding their feet, so you may have to be patient.

As I write this Windsave, for example, are still in the process of producing a pack especially to assist with applying for planning permission. Presumably, this will include a scale diagram of their turbine which can be easily copied onto the diagram of your house. They are also a month or two off producing an independent report on the noise produced by their WS1000, which will be essential in persuading neighbours and planning officers alike that this is a device suitable for a domestic rooftop.

Filling out the form

Once you've actually got the plans sorted, you've done the hardest part. Just make sure that you tick all the boxes. It's not that complicated, just a little time-consuming. Our council, for example, asks for the following:

- ordnance survey plan of the site (four copies)

- the elevation diagram (four copies)

- the completed application form (four copies).

The important thing to remember when applying for a wind turbine is to provide plenty of supporting material. Ideally this should be:

- examples of other approvals for this make and model of turbine;

- information about the turbine, including the independent noise and vibration survey;

- what you've done to consult your neighbours, what objections they've raised, and how you plan to resolve those objections.

Essentially, you need to show that you recognise that there are issues surrounding turbines, but the turbine you want to put in is well suited to your property, and you've done everything you can to keep your neighbours happy. Which brings us on to the next section...

Consulting the neighbours

If you have not already done so, at this stage you should consult your neighbours. In this context, your neighbours are anyone who may object to the planning permission. And while this step is not a *requirement* of the planning permission process, there are a number of reasons to do this.

Firstly, you should be aware that your planning application is a public document, so there is no way you can slip this development past your neighbours!

Secondly, as with anything new, they are bound to have concerns and reservations. It is far better to handle them sitting in the living room over a cup of tea, than through objections and appeals in the planning process. Each objection should be examined carefully. Although many objections may be spurious, this doesn't mean that they shouldn't be considered. Your neighbours may have perfectly legitimate objections to raise, which can be taken into account at the initial stage.

Noise and vibration

Noise is of major concern to most people. It is essential to have the full statistics about your turbine on hand when handling your neighbours' objections. The planning authority works on the 'worst case scenario'. For a wind turbine, this is a quiet summer night, when your closest neighbours have the window open, and there is just enough wind to turn the turbine. Any turbine manufacturer worth their salt should have an independent noise and vibration report which you can get with a few persistent phonecalls.

The official ruling on what is allowed for a turbine is contained in a very large and complex set of documents published by the DTI. Together they form a publication called 'The assessment and rating of noise from wind farms' (URN No: 96/1192). If you're really brave, you can download it from here: http://www.dti.gov.uk/energy/sources/renewables/publications/page21743.html

But rather than wade through this publication, you're far better off getting your turbine company to establish credibility on your behalf – hence the independent noise and vibration report.

Other objections which are of equal priority, but much harder to gauge, are the effect on TV reception, and the visual impact. Of course, you can't handle every objection, but if you can go some way to showing that you've taken your neighbours' feelings into account, you will have built a strong case for approval.

9. Apply for grants

We will assume for the purposes of this section, that you are applying for a grant from the LCBP here. In all likelihood, they're the best people to go to as they specialise in funding for renewable projects. The process to go through to satisfy the funders are:

1. Take basic energy saving steps (see 1 above).

2. Get a quote from an approved installer for an approved appliance.

3. Fill in the application form.

4. After the work is complete, fill in an 'installer completion certificate'.

You can either fill in an application online at the LCBP website or you can download the form and post it.

Applying online

To get to the online form go to http://www.lowcarbonbuildings.org.uk then click on 'How to apply', and follow the links. If the funds for the current month have already run out, you can get to the link for the application form here: http://www.lowcarbonbuildings.org.uk/lcbp/application/applicationForm 1Public.action

Sadly, only £12.7 million has been allocated for householders for the LCBP, capped at £0.5 million per month, so the message isn't getting through. Whether the scheme will be extended or not remains to be seen. Considering the EU's goals of cutting carbon emissions by 20 per cent by every member state by 2020, a lot more than this small sum is going to be required. Although by 2020, fossil fuel depletion may well have forced this reduction on us.

10. Install your system

Finally, you are now ready to have your system installed. Good luck!

BUYING GREEN ELECTRICITY

There will be plenty of situations where you need to buy electricity from the grid. Even if you do generate your own electricity, it may not cover all your needs. So most of us, at some time or another, are going to need to buy electricity. But how can we buy carbon neutral electricity?

Many power companies around these days offer a green tariff. But what is a green tariff? And just how green is it?

To persuade us that the energy being offered is green, power companies offer one of the following three options:

- green source

- green fund

- carbon offset.

Green source

The first, and best option is to offer electricity from renewable sources. This way you can be sure that the electricity you use is carbon neutral:

> 'For every unit of electricity you use, a supplier guarantees to buy a percentage of electricity (from 10 per cent to 100 per cent) from a renewable generator which uses wind, small hydro-electric, biomass, tidal and wave power, geothermal and/or solar.' (www.energywatch.org.uk/help_ and_advice/green_tariffs/ tariff_types.asp)

Note that even then, you do need to check what *percentage* of the electricity you use is from a green source, as it will need to be 100 per cent to be truly carbon neutral. Having said that, even 10 per cent is better than 0 per cent!

To be absolutely sure that your electricity is carbon neutral, you can always switch to a green power company such as Ecotricity, Good Energy or Green Energy (see Useful Information – Green Power Companies). Bear in mind however, that you will have to pay a premium for this electricity.

Green fund

There are two main types of green fund:

1. New renewables; which are designed to support the construction of new renewable generation sources such as wind farms, solar power and so on.

2. Other environmental; which are designed to support environmental causes or new research and development projects.

The point to note here is that the electricity you are buying *is not carbon neutral*. Although these funds may be a worthy cause, and may in future lead to more wind turbines, they do not in themselves reduce global warming. Since you will be paying a premium for these funds, why not either donate the money to a charity such as Friends of the Earth, or even use it to save up for a wind turbine? This would be just as positive a difference, and you would know yourself where your money ended up.

Carbon offset

This is probably the least defensible 'green' tariff. The idea is that the supplier makes a donation to a carbon reduction project – either in the UK or abroad. In a similar vein to a green fund, your electricity is still not carbon neutral. This practice of 'offsetting' is especially dangerous because it encourages people to think that it is actually carbon neutral, when it isn't. Any number of forests are not going to offset the effects of burning fossil fuels, especially coal.

This modern trend is basically greenwash: The Energy Saving Trust says it is '…the potential gap between agreeing in public with the consensus, and not attempting to do anything about it.'

The same applies here as applies to the 'green fund' above. Why not put your money to use elsewhere?

WIND TURBINE COMMUNITY SCHEMES

Getting a turbine for your home and generating your own electricity is all well and good, but there are a number of situations where it simply isn't going to be practical. Whether you rent a property, you're in a conservation area, or the property just isn't suitable; whatever the reason, it's not always possible to install a device where you live.

> Just because you can't site a turbine on your property doesn't mean you can't generate electricity – just not on your roof.

Using a grid connection means that a turbine can be connected just about any-where. Electricity can then be sold to the grid at the wholesale price, and bought back at retail in the same way as if the turbine was on your roof. Having the device actually at your own home can become a non-issue. And once you widen the location for a turbine, you automatically increase its possible size. This has a further advantage. Remember that when we were discussing choosing a make and model, we looked at the cost per kW capacity as being the guideline for making our selection. Well it turns out that as turbines increase in size, the cost per kW drops dramatically. The most cost-effective way to set up a wind turbine is to set up a large turbine project and have a number of stakeholders, each taking a share of the electricity produced. In this way, each person only puts in a small amount, but reaps the cost-effectiveness of owning a large, efficient turbine.

Community groups already out there

The term 'community' wind turbine can be confusing. It can mean a group of people in a local area who all wish to share a turbine for generating electricity, each putting in a certain investment to the scheme. However, investors can be anywhere in the country and don't need to share the same geographic area. Often, when a turbine share offer is extended to outside the area where the turbine is situated, preference is given for those living closest.

In the UK, there are very few community-owned turbines. Most are owned exclusively by a single company. There are exceptions, however. Baywind, for example, has set up a number of turbines which are owned by groups of people. These are owned and operated as a commercial project, and pay dividends to their members. Find out more via the website www.baywind.co.uk

Staying the distance

But as the size of the project increases, so does the organisational load. Be warned. Setting up a community owned turbine is a very time-consuming task, and is not to be taken lightly. If you want a quick and easy solution to your electricity supply, this is *not* the way to go. Having said this, a large project such as a community turbine can have tremendous benefits, but you must be prepared to go the whole distance.

Setting up and running a community turbine project could be the subject for a book on its own, so what follows is nothing more than an overview of this relatively new area.

Type of company

The first task is to create a legal vessel for the idea. There are a number of different types of company which will fulfil this role. The main types are:

- Private Limited Company
- Company Limited by Guarantee
- Cooperative.

Private Limited Company

The first choice is a Private Limited Company. These are owned by a number of shareholders, who each pay money for shares and receive dividends each year for each share they hold. Shares also limit the liability of a company, in that it cannot lose more money than is put in. If you invest for example, £500 in a company, and it owes millions, you cannot have your house seized to pay the company's debts – you can only lose the £500 that was invested in the first place. An accountant can set up a limited company for around £250.

Company Limited by Guarantee

A Company Limited by Guarantee has no shares, and does not declare dividends, but is still limited to a small amount. This might be as small as £1. A good example here is a charity. If you were trying to set up a turbine which would benefit your village hall or school, this might be the way to go. Although the turbine company wouldn't be able to pay out any profits, it would be able to run the turbine effectively, which could then provide free electricity to a beneficiary, such as the village hall or school. The charges made by accountants vary, but setting up these two different company types shouldn't have radically different costs.

Cooperative

The third type of organisation which might be suitable is a cooperative. A good example here is Baywind, which owns and operates wind turbines to the benefit of its members. However, cooperatives are a special type of organisation and, typically, would not pay out a dividend. An example of a cooperative might be a working man's club, where the members benefit by having an economical social club run at cost. But no profits would normally be paid out. It can be quite expensive to set up a cooperative (one estimate ran at £750 – £1,500), and involves the cooperative being ratified and regularly audited. Cooperatives cannot be set up automatically; an application must be made to create one. This takes time, money and does not guarantee success. If you do want to go down this particular road, then you may want to consider purchasing a copy of Baywind's legal articles, and using them as a model. This can be done through their spin-off company, www.energy4all.co.uk

Energy4All

It is worth mentioning Energy4All at this stage. It is a professional company which specialises in helping set up community cooperatives for the purpose of developing commercial wind farms. The advantage is that it has done this sort of work before and knows the pitfalls. So if you're wary of setting up a turbine project without any experience, then it may be worth contacting Energy4All, to see if it can help you get started.

Get professional advice

This brief overview of the legal vehicles available is very simplified, and is not a substitute for consulting an accountant. Most accountants won't charge for a consultation, only for the work that results from that consultation. So there is no reason not to go and talk to a professional.

Grants

Once you have set up your group as a legal entity, you can then apply for a bank account and grants. One of the nice things about a community project is that you qualify for all manner of assistance. You can apply for funding from hundreds of different sources (whole books have been written on this subject). Essentially, it is important to know exactly what you are applying for, what the money will be used for and that your group meets the funder's requirements. So a good application might be for £5,000, for example, for legal fees from a carbon neutral trust.

The applications process has become more sophisticated over the years, and you must be prepared to state your case carefully in the application form. You will probably need a referee to argue on your behalf, and have evidence such as quotes for the work to be done. But do persist!

> Setting up a community turbine is an excellent cause, and there are literally millions of pounds available to the right organisations.

The only expense you are unlikely to gain funding for is the initial setup with the accountant. Since you will only exist as a group of like-minded friends at this stage, funders will be reluctant to make you an award due to the high risk of fraud. But for everything else you have an open field – if you don't ask, you don't get!

Low Carbon Buildings Programme

The grant from the Low Carbon Buildings Programme has now been expanded to include businesses. The LCBP explains on its website (www.lowcarbonbuildings. org.uk).

'The stream 2 fund is comprised of two categories:

■ Stream 2A – to be allocated over seven funding rounds (and one reserve round) Maximum grant of £100k or 40–50 per cent of total costs (excl.

VAT). There will be quarterly deadlines for stream 2A applications. Apply now by completing a pre-registration form.

▪ Stream 2B – to be allocated over three funding rounds (and one reserve round) Maximum grant of £1m or 40-50 per cent of total costs (excl. VAT). Deadlines for applications will be twice a year. Apply now for a building assessment form by pre-registering.'

It seems incredible, but profit-making businesses are now allowed to apply for up to 50 per cent of a scheme, which is only capped at £1m. So set your sights high!

Other finance

Although grants can provide a welcome lifeline for a turbine project, often you'll want to involve others as investors either to make the purchase more secure, or to widen the range of turbines you can afford.

There are a number of ways that finance can be raised (this list is by no means exhaustive).

Fundraising

For a project which is going to benefit the whole community, such as a turbine for the school, this approach can be very successful. However, it is important to know who will be the beneficiaries in any project, and this will be of keen interest to anyone donating to such a fund. Often this is suitable for raising smaller sums such as the initial accountant's bill.

Investors

Like members of a cooperative, investors can pay a membership and they will then be eligible to receive dividends once the turbine is fully operational. It is important here to consider who your investors are likely to be, and what their interests will be. A simple business plan showing the projected income and expenditure of the business in its first and subsequent years can go a long way to answering initial queries.

Commercial borrowing

Taking out a loan against your turbine is a serious step to take. And because it is a 'fringe' business, it may be problematic securing finance in this manner. Banks will want assurances, and will likely want the loan to be secured against an asset, so this isn't something to take lightly. The important questions here are *why* a loan needs to be taken out, and *how* that loan will be repaid.

According to Energy4All (www.energy4all.co.uk):

'If the project is attractive a bank will lend up to 80 per cent of the project costs, subject to due diligence and a charge over the assets.'

If the majority of the funding for a project is to come from commercial borrowing, then a projected cash flow analysis – what goes in, and what comes out – is essential. This is to ensure that the costs of the business will be met, and that any loans can be serviced.

Settling on a location

Once you have an organisation and potential funding, you can now go about the process of setting up your turbine. The first issue is the site. Where you plan to put the turbine will depend very much on the emphasis of your group. Of course, there is nothing to stop your London group siting its turbine in Galway. But it might become difficult to discuss matters with local land owners, or objectors, for example. A good place to start is with local land owners with lots of windy land. Obviously, you do need to be tactful when discussing the matter, but you may be surprised to find your proposal very well received. After all, a turbine takes very little from the land, and can provide a strong profit incentive.

> The location here is very important. Not only does the wind yield need to be taken carefully into account, but also the distance to the grid.

Is there a farm nearby with mains electricity, where the turbine can be hooked into? To get a quote for grid connection for a location you need to contact your local DNO (See Useful Information). When speaking to ours, the range quoted was from £5,000 to £50,000. Also look at ease of access from the road for plant vehicles. Remember, this thing is going to need foundations and to be hoisted into place with a crane!

Energy4All's website says:

'You will need to calculate the distance to the nearest grid connection point and assess the cost of this. To do this you will need to contact your Distribution Network Operator (DNO) or contact a consultant to do this on your behalf. To commission a system study will cost between £6 to 15k but a one off consultation may provide a good guide to start with on spare capacity on the line and any work that may be required to reinforce the lines.'

Obviously, the cost here will depend on the size of your project, but location with respect to wind yield and suitability for the grid is an important consideration.

Legal agreement with a land owner

Having found one or more sympathetic land owners, the next step is to make the agreement more formal by involving a solicitor. This is where you may wish to start applying for a grant, as obviously solicitors will charge for their services. However bureaucratic this step may seem, it is essential. There is no use in applying for planning permission on a local farmer's land, and battling through all the protests, only to find that the farmer has signed an agreement with a commercial wind developer!

A further complication here is that this type of agreement is highly specialised. Unless you live in an area crowded with wind turbines, you are unlikely to find a solicitor who is experienced in these matters, and may have to look further afield.

Again, organisations such as the British Wind Energy Association (BWEA, http://www.bwea.com) or Energy4All may be able to supply you with a contact, if your local solicitors are unable to help.

Selecting your turbine

The same rules apply here as to buying a micro-turbine for your home, but on a much bigger scale. Again you are looking for the best price per kW, but now you can open up the field from 50kW anywhere up to perhaps 250kW and beyond. This gives you far greater flexibility in terms of make and model. However, you still need to remember that only certain turbines and certain installers attract funding, so be sure to check with the LCBP to ensure that the turbine you select will be fully funded. See Useful Information for more details on approved appliances and installers.

You don't even need to stick to new turbines – you can also look at second-hand turbines. These can be had quite cheaply, with only a few years on the clock. Typically, this happens when a new wind farm has been set up with several small turbines to ensure the wind yield is present. They are then replaced with much larger turbines and the smaller devices are sold second-hand. The internet is the best place to look for second-hand turbines (but buyer beware!).

Finally, when you are buying a large-scale turbine, don't lose sight of the fact that you are engaged in major engineering works. Even once the turbine is in place, it will still need to be maintained by qualified engineers. To find engineers suitable for this, contact the BWEA (British Wind Energy Association).

Wind surveys: do I need one?

This depends on your view of the site, and how you will raise finance for it. If you and your investors are willing to take the site at face value, then you don't necessarily need a wind survey. If you do need one, it consists of installing an anemometer and recording the results. It can be a lot of money to raise for a project which hasn't even got started yet, and the simple economics of the situation may rule this out completely. However, if you are able to gain funding, then this can be a very useful step to take. Obviously, the larger the turbine you are considering, the more sensible such a precaution becomes. If your project is going to cost half a million pounds, then spending £12,000 on a wind survey becomes a lot more prudent. Also, if you are looking at obtaining some of the money for the project from a funder, or even a bank, then a wind survey can help to establish credibility in the eyes of those providing the finance and show that the investment isn't going to be wasted money.

Commercial wind developments will almost always commission a wind survey of at least one point on a potential wind farm site, even if it consists of a very small turbine (e.g. 5kW). Since such developments are wholly on a commercial footing, they also tend to insure themselves against low yields of wind. Wind insurance! This type of insurance will pay out in the case of a very low wind yield in a year, enabling repayments on a loan to be made. Before applying for insurance of this type, a wind survey is essential.

So the answer to whether you need a wind survey or not really depends on how much it matters if the wind blows or not. If the yield of your site was radically below your estimates, would it matter to your plans? If the answer to this is yes, then chances are you will need to get a wind survey.

Making your planning application

Like the home turbine process, this is perhaps the most arduous step of all. But in the case of a large turbine, instead of ensuring that the objections of your immediate neighbours are met, you need to deal with communities and organisations. As with a micro-turbine, if at all possible you should find out who your potential objectors are initially, and meet with them in a private setting to discuss your proposal informally. Considering the money and time that may go into obtaining planning permission for a community turbine, it is prudent to get informal approval from any potential objection group, before going to the official application stage.

People who apply for planning permission for a wind turbine tend to come against a local protest group at some point, and often there is a public debate involving the local commuinity.

Common objections

These are the most common objections:

1. Radar interference

Surprisingly, one of the most common objectors to a large turbine development is the RAF. Interference with radar ranks highly on the list of objections and is very credible. This should be one of your first checkpoints. An inital approach would be to write to the RAF base involved, and outline your plans. This will save a lot of wasted time and effort further down the road.

2. Visual intrusion

This is a highly subjective, but perfectly valid objection. What does or does not constitute 'unacceptable visual intrusion' will depend on your council's planning department. The only way to assess whether your development will fall foul of this objection is to contact your council.

3. Noise

As has already been discussed, a noise report for the turbine in question should be in your hand, and the hands of any potential objectors, before even beginning to fill out the application form.

4. Environmental damage

It seems incredible that a device for reducing directly global warming could be painted as an environmental hazard, but that is sometimes the case. To install a large wind turbine, a suitable area has to be dug out and filled with concrete to form the foundations, as well as suitable trenches for the cables to be laid. The larger the turbine, the more likely that the planning department is to insist on a full Environmental Impact Assessment by an independent third party, which can be extremely costly.

5. Conservation areas

Some areas will have protected status, and rightly so. It is important to take into account areas and buildings which have been designated as National Heritage sites, and conservation areas. Rather than fight such designations, it may be prudent to locate the turbine to another area. Obviously, this is going to depend very much on the circumstances of the application.

6. Transmitter interference

Other than the RAF there are a number of civil communications channels that may be affected by a wind turbine, in particular TV transmitters and mobile phone masts. The landscape is entwined with such masts (which often have their applications swiftly approved by central government!), and a large turbine may interfere with any one of them. If there are any such masts in the area, it would be wise to contact the owners at the earliest opportunity.

Other objections

Of course there are any number of objections which may be voiced at the planning stage, but the ones represented so far are the most credible. Other objections which you may encounter along the way are that wind turbines:

- kill birds

- distract drivers

- frighten horses

- are a health hazard

- damage house prices

- damage tourism

- don't produce much energy.

These are all myths, as outlined on www.dti.gov.uk in the section 'Wind power: 10 myths explained'. If truth be told wind turbines are the best chance Britain has to produce long-term sustainable energy. These myths, and others like them, are often to be heard at public meetings and on radio debates.

Bringing it all together

When you look at all the obstacles facing a community wind turbine project, it's small wonder that very few ever conclude successfully. But if you want to set up a turbine in your community, don't be put off by all the nay-sayers. The more projects that are set up, the more turbines we are likely to see further down the road.

Assuming you have planning permission, the final step is installation. There may be issues surrounding finance here in the final stages. This is because grants from the Low Carbon Buildings Programme are only paid *after* a turbine is set up, but must be applied for *before*. This bureaucratic gap can sometimes cause a mini financial crisis, if you are not prepared for it. You may be able to talk to the suppliers and installers of the turbine for help in this respect, and offer them payment only when the grant cheque clears, as part of the contract. Any company that deals with turbines on a regular basis is likely to be familiar with the grant system, and may be understanding. Failing this, you can always get a short-term loan, or an overdraft, to cover this shortfall. But bear in mind that this will accumulate interest, even if for a short time, and without income from the turbine this can represent another item in the liabilities column of the balance sheet.

All that remains to be said now is 'good luck!'.

OUTPUTS

What this section comes down to is: how can we cut our use of electricity? There are two routes here:

- by using efficient devices
- by using less energy.

Let's look at each in turn.

Using efficient devices

Low energy light bulbs

At the top of the list of efficient devices must be the low energy light bulb. In no other way can such a dramatic saving be made for as little as 95p. Really, high energy bulbs should be outlawed! Using high energy bulbs is just like driving a huge 4x4 when you don't need to.

The savings on low energy bulbs are amazing. They consume one fifth of the energy, and last eight to ten times longer than conventional bulbs. If you hunt around, especially at local DIY stores, you can often pick them up for only a little more than a conventional bulb.

So make this number one on your list. You'd be crazy not to.

Big electrical appliances

Once you've added low energy bulbs to your home, the next items you should be looking at are the big appliances. Typically, the biggest energy hog in your house is going to be the fridge freezer. This is because it is on all the time.

Ideally, you would scrap your old fridge freezer immediately and rush out and buy an A++ rated model. This would save you £45 per year according to the Energy Saving Trust. However, you may want to look at new models now, but only replace the old one when it comes to the end of its life. If this is the case, then you could consider a Savaplug.

A Savaplug (www.savawatt.com) is a unique energy saving device which simply replaces the existing plug on your fridge freezer and saves you typically 20 per cent. The RRP is £24.99, so they are well worth investigating. However, they will not work with a number of makes and models, so make sure that yours is compatible. It is well worth a phone call to ensure this.

The other big energy hogs are the electric cooker, tumble dryer, washing machine and dishwasher. If you do really need one, each of these can be bought as an A+ model, and will naturally save you energy, and money.

Using less energy

There are a thousand tips and tricks for using less electricity, so much so that cataloguing them all could be a book in itself. But here's some of the most useful:

Fridge freezer

- Try to open the fridge freezer as little as possible. If you are cooking, for example, get all the ingredients out at once.

- Keep the condenser coils dust-free.

- Keep it well filled with items.

Cooking

- Use lids on your saucepans so the heat doesn't escape.

- When possible only use one hob. For example cook one-pot meals, or move pans between the hobs.

- Heat water for cooking in the kettle first – it's more efficient.

- An electric hob stays hot long after they are turned off, so try turning it off (or down) a few minutes before the end of the cooking time.

- Completely cover the hob to use all the heat.

- Don't open the oven until the food has finished cooking.

Laundry

- Try washing on a lower temperature cycle.

- Wash only full loads.

- Try to use the tumble dryer as little as possible, and try the solar powered alternative – the clothes line!

A+ washers are great for this. They can be set for short cycles (some as little as 29 minutes!), lower temperatures, and even control the maximum spin speed.

All the rest

- If something's not being used, unplug it at the wall – never mind leaving it on standby! To aid this, use an adapter with several sockets, and one switch.

- Have a shower instead of a bath, as it uses less energy and water. If you have carbon neutral heating, try a mixer shower which will use what's in the tank first, then start using electricity.

■ Try running appliances such as washers, dryers and dishwashers at night on cheap electricity. Is this carbon neutral? Well, wind turbines run at night.

■ Electric lawn mowers are more efficient than petrol mowers. And of course push mowers are truly carbon neutral.

These are all common sense tips which can gradually lower your consumption. The tricky part is getting your whole family behind the idea.

CONCLUSION

It seems that every week there is some new development in this area of the carbon neutral movement, what with politicians putting up turbines to grab the headlines. The danger of writing a chapter like this is that it will probably be out of date by the time you're reading it! The grants available were completely revised while it was being written, so check your sources.

One of the boldest moves has been by Edinburgh city council to allow turbines without planning permission. So if you live in Edinburgh, there's no excuses!

Gradually the government is getting around to talking about global warming, but despite the rhetoric, very little seems to be happening. When you consider that only £18 million has been allotted for the householders stream of the LCBP, it gives you some idea of how little thought this is being given. To put it in perspective, to put an extra lane on the M1 is set to cost nearly £2 billion!

Despite the government's general unwillingness to act, pressure is mounting for Britain to become more carbon neutral, and this should translate into it becoming gradually easier to get planning permission for turbines of all sizes.

Hopefully this chapter should have made things clearer, and although it can be a daunting process to go through, it is another step towards becoming carbon neutral.

GRANTS AVAILABLE

Householders

The following grants are available from the Low Carbon Buildings Programme (LCBP) for householders. Although it may be possible to attract funding from other areas, e.g. lottery funding, the LCBP should be your first stop. See www.lowcarbonbuildings.org.uk/how/householders

Solar photovoltaics: Maximum of £2,000 per kW of installed capacity, subject to an overall maximum of £2,500 or 50 per cent of the relevant eligible costs, whichever is the lower.

Wind turbines: Maximum of £1,000 per kW of installed capacity, subject to an overall maximum of £2,500 or 30 per cent of the relevant eligible costs, whichever is the lower.

Small hydro: Maximum of £1,000 per kW of installed capacity, subject to an overall maximum of £2,500 or 30 per cent of the relevant eligible costs, whichever is the lower.

Businesses and SMEs (small and medium enterprises)

The stream 2 fund is comprised of two categories (see www.lowcarbon-buildings.org.uk/how/stream2):

▣ Stream 2A – to be allocated over seven funding rounds (and one reserve round). Maximum grant of £100k or 40-50 per cent of total costs (excl. VAT). There will be quarterly deadlines for stream 2A applications. Apply now by completing a pre-registration form.

▣ Stream 2B – to be allocated over three funding rounds (and one reserve round). Maximum grant of £1m or 40-50 per cent of total costs (excl. VAT). Deadlines for applications will be twice a year. Apply now for a building assessment form by pre-registering.

4

Water

INTRODUCTION

Here we are going to talk about one of the most difficult areas to unhook from. Recycling your own water is an expensive business and several solutions require more land than most people have, such as a reed bed. Not only does such a system need to be a certain size but also, for obvious reasons, needs to be a certain *distance* from your property. Especially in summer. In fact, by the time you get done with this section, you might actually start being glad that you're paying your water bill and that you don't have to organise the whole shebang yourself! When you look at the figures for setting up your own water recycling system for a house you'll soon see how reasonable £200–300 a year is.

But there are a lot of aspects of recycling water, as we shall see. It might not be possible to recycle everything, but it is still possible to do something. For example, did you know that one the largest parts of the average household's water usage is from flushing the loo? Does it really need to be done with clean, drinking water? You'll soon see that big savings can be made by just attacking one or two parts of the problem.

You might be surprised to see a section about water: What's that got to do with being carbon neutral? Do the water companies really use a lot of fossil fuel? Surprisingly, the answer is yes.

> 'Over 10 billion litres of sewage are produced every day in England and Wales. It takes approximately 6.34 gigawatt hours of energy to treat this volume of sewage, almost 1 per cent of the average daily electricity consumption of England and Wales.' (www.parliament.uk)

This amount of energy is not without its carbon cost, and beyond this we need to address this section in terms of sustainability.

A load of jargon

When people who know what they're on about start talking about water recycling, they use terms like 'black water' and 'grey water'. Below is a list of terms you may not be familiar with.

Potable water: drinking water.

Black water: raw sewage. This is the stuff that gets flushed out of your loo.

Grey water: all other waste water: what goes down the plughole. It's bath water, washing machine outflow and other waste.

Primary treatment: the stage of sewage treatment: this separates out the solids from the liquids.

Secondary treatment: after separation: this treats the liquids that drain out of the primary treatment.

INPUTS

WATER USAGE

What is our water used for? The amount of water used by each household, and the uses it is put to, will of course vary. But the average household uses over a week (see www.freerain.co.uk):

Item	Litres	Per cent
Toilet flush	165	33
Personal washing	120	24
Drinking & cooking	75	15
Washing machine	60	12
Washing up	45	9
Garden & car	35	7

It seems incredible that a third of our water usage is for flushing the loo. Even worse, it's drinking water. This seems like such an obvious target for reducing and recycling, it's a wonder it's not done more often. Many people, myself included, would probably have thought bathing would have been at the top of the list.

But it's worth bearing in mind that these are just estimates and different sources will give different figures. If you are *seriously* considering recycling your own water, you'll want to make more accurate measurements.

Should I get a water meter fitted?

Ideally yes, everyone should get one fitted. However, you ought to be aware how much this is going to cost you, as you could be in for a shock! Just as I urge folks to calculate their electricity usage, and reduce it before getting a wind turbine, so I would urge anyone thinking of getting a water meter fitted to calculate their water usage and reduce any waste here first. If you do phone up your water company, they will go through the approximate cost first and ensure that you understand what it entails. Remember that getting a water meter fitted won't do anything for the environment, only *the way in which you're charged*. What actually makes the difference here is reducing the amount of water your household uses.

It would have been nice to include a system here to calculate how much you'd be charged with a water meter, but it's not that simple! Different water companies charge in different ways. The charge can also be reduced if you only require an input (i.e. you're recycling all your waste water and sewage), or if you don't require any surface water drainage (disposal of rainwater). Either way it is difficult to pin down exactly what your usage will cost.

However, you can calculate the *amount* you use. An excellent water calculator can be found on the BBC website (www.bbc.co.uk) by searching for 'water calculator'. Rather than try to calculate a cost, this calculates the amount you use.

Alternatively, you can use the do it manually using the following table. This table started life as the 'Water Calculator Workings' from the BBC site. However, some items have been removed and others added.

Detailed water usage

Item	Usage (litres)	Source
Shower	7 per minute	Waterwise
Power shower	12 per minute	Waterwise
Bath	80 – 90	Various
Brush teeth – water on	10	MyInternet
Brush teeth – water off	1	MyInternet
Wash hands or face	5	MyInternet
Toilet flush	4.5 – 13	Various
Running tap	6 per minute	Thames Water
Washing up	10 (2×5 litre bowl)	Various
Dishwasher (modern)	15	Waterwise
Washing machine (modern)	50	Environment Agency
Hosepipe	500 per hour	Waterwise

For example, if in one day I have a bath, brush my teeth (with the water off) twice, wash my face twice, flush the toilet three times, and do the washing up once, then my water usage might be a total of 120 litres per day:

Bath	80
Brush teeth – water off	2
Wash my face twice	10 (2 × 5 litres)
Flush toilet three times	18 (3 × 6 litres)
Washing up	10
Total:	120

This adds up to 43,800 litres over a year.

TYPES OF SYSTEM

Water butt

Really, this system couldn't be simpler and as far as inputs go it has to be the first that anyone should try. A section of drainpipe is replaced with a special collector which sends rainwater down a pipe into a large plastic barrel. The collected water can then be used for watering the garden or washing the car. There's really nothing more to it than that. There are dozens of different types available from DIY shops, the internet or your water company. They start at around £20–30, with a stand for around £10. Diverter kits are also available which allow you to divert rainwater from a drainpipe straight into your water butt. These cost between £10–20.

Rainwater harvesting

This is perhaps one of the most exciting and romantic ideas – getting all your water for free, off the roof. But it isn't as simple as that. Water collected from the roof is actually only suitable for a few purposes:

- flushing the loo
- washing clothes
- watering the garden
- washing the car.

So before looking at harvesting rainwater, we need to look at what we are going to use it for. As we've seen, flushing the loo is potentially the biggest area for savings.

How does it work?

In theory they're quite simple. Rainwater is collected via your downpipes in the same way as a water butt would, but instead of going into your water butt the rainwater goes into a very large container, usually buried underground to save space. Then, in the same way that mains water is pumped up to the header tank at the top of the house, rainwater is pumped up to a separate tank. So when you flush the loo, for example, instead of drawing water from the mains header tank, it is drawn from the rainwater header tank. You can also get an outside tap fitted to the rainwater tank for the garden or car.

How much does it cost?

The issue with rainwater harvesting systems is the same for a lot of the systems mentioned – money. Such a system can easily set you back £2–3,000. And when you consider that an *entire year's supply* of water is only £2–300, this isn't going to pay itself back any time soon unless water suddenly becomes very expensive. Does this mean no one should bother? No, it's just that there are dozens of other items to spend this amount of money on that would help reduce carbon emissions and enable people to lead more sustainable lives.

As the Centre for Alternative Technology puts it (www.cat.org.uk):

'A rainwater harvesting system to provide toilet flushing for a 3 or 4 bedroom house is likely to cost at least £2,000. It may be possible to install a simpler gravity-fed system, for a ground-floor toilet and garden watering, for less then £1,000. Because these systems are fairly expensive, the payback time can be very long. In fact a system might never recover its costs if parts need replacing before savings are realised – especially if your water is not metered.'

Grey water recycling

This one could really qualify under inputs *and* outputs, as it covers the output of grey water, and also the input of water for flushing the loo. But the principle is so similar to the rainwater harvesting system that I thought it would be suited to this section.

Simply put, a grey water recycling system runs in a similar fashion to the rain harvesting system above, in that waste water is collected in a large tank, then pumped up to a header tank, before being used to flush the toilet or water the garden. The biggest difference between this system and the rainwater harvesting system is that the input to the system is grey water, rather than rainwater. The only restriction that this causes is that some plants may not fare well when watered with grey water, and obviously you can't use grey water to wash your clothes. However, it can still be used to flush the loo, the biggest cost of water.

Drawbacks

Essentially this has similar drawbacks to a rainwater harvesting system, such as the expense in setting such a system up. Also, the effect on the environment may not be positive in the long run:

'Commercially available grey water recycling systems use disinfectants that are often very energy intensive to produce – and which may also cause problems if you have a private sewage treatment system. All independently published case studies of installed systems have shown running costs higher than that of mains water supply. Given the infrastructure requirements and the disinfectant doses needed, it is very difficult to see these systems as environmentally friendly, especially for individual households.' (www.cat.org.uk)

The reason why these systems are not entirely suitable in Britain is simply that we are lucky enough to have a plentiful supply of rainwater. Despite the environmental effects, countries with much drier climates would probably benefit from these systems a great deal. In Australia, for example, such systems may become essential as clean drinking water becomes more scarce.

Boreholes

These are the modern equivalent of a well where you source your own water supply. However, it affects the amount of water in the garden soil, or immediate area, and the setup is quite expensive. Prices can start from about £6,000.

Even at £300 per year for your water bill, this is still a 20-year payback, and even then you must somehow dispose of your grey and black water. This is not a straightforward proposition!

OUTPUTS

DISPOSING OF SEWAGE

There are several systems for disposing of sewage (also known as black water), but none of them are without their issues or expense. Given the previously mentioned low cost of a water bill, these are probably only suitable where connection to the mains is impractical, such as in isolated rural areas. But for the sake of completeness, the systems are outlined below.

Composting toilet

Probably one of the simplest systems available. You can actually make your own quite easily and *The Humanure Handbook* is happy to tell you how! Essentially, you need a large, plastic bucket which can be easily removed and replaced with another. Fitting on top of this is a standard loo seat with a hinged top, so that the buckets can easily be taken out. Every time you go to the loo, you throw in a handful of sawdust which creates a ready-made bucket of compost material.

Apart from the initial reaction of horror, this is actually quite a simple system, provided you don't mind lugging a bucket of waste outside with you every few weeks!

The catch with a composting toilet is where the composting takes place. The process can take up to two years before it is ready to be safely used on your garden, and even then you are likely to produce far more than is needed for the average garden!

Septic tank

This is the first stage in the traditional treatment of sewage – settlement. A septic tank allows solids and liquids to separate. The solids need removing and taking away periodically, whereas the liquids flow out to a secondary treatment. Typically this is a leachfield: perforated pipes lead out of the septic tank, and the liquids seep out into gravel beds. There micro-organisms remove and digest solids, before it eventually ends up in our groundwater.

Such a system would allow you to dispense with the mains water for sewage disposal, but the solids from your septic tank would still need to be disposed of in some way every so often, so how far ahead does this get you? Given the expense of such a system, I'd probably be more inclined to try out the composting toilet!

Reed beds

At some point in the past you may have heard about reed beds being used for sewage treatment. This is a secondary stage treatment system only, and is really only suitable on a small scale. The Hockerton Housing Project of four households, for example, uses a reed bed treatment system. The reed bed's roots and micro-organisms effectively do the work of the gravel bed in the leachfield system (above). It makes the effluent safe to be allowed into the groundwater.

Disadvantages

It is only a secondary treatment system, so the solids still need to be dealt with in the same manner as they would with a septic tank.

A reed bed requires a significant area of land, similar to many of the systems mentioned here for the treatment of black water. It needs an area much bigger than the back garden that many people have available – probably about the same area as a swimming pool. It's also not likely to be cheap.

Advantages

Having said all this, the advantages should be kept in mind. Principally, a reed bed system requires no chemicals or electricity, other than perhaps a small pump to get the water from the septic tank, if necessary. It also produces very clean water, so clean in fact that even chemical pollutants and heavy metals can be removed. With a suitable filtration system, the water can even be returned to potable water.

SAVING WATER

To be fair, when you look at the expense involved in the sophisticated systems detailed in this chapter, most of us are better off simply following some basic guidelines for saving water.

Flushing the toilet

If you take nothing else away with you from this chapter, take this: a third of all our water use goes down the toilet. So unless you're going to set up a system for disposing of your own sewage, as outlined above, then the biggest single saving you can make is to reduce the amount of water you flush down the toilet.

Calculating your cistern size

The first thing to do here is to find out how much water your cistern actually holds.

1. Take off the cistern lid – *carefully*.

2. Hold up the float, so that the cistern doesn't fill up (you will need someone to help you).

3. Carefully measure out the water with a measuring jug. Make sure you don't damage the float or ball valve.

The results from this little exercise can be quite astounding. Measurements will vary anything from six to 12 litres. Given that it only takes about six litres to flush a loo, a 12 litre toilet is wasting an awful lot. Remember this isn't even recycled water, it's pure drinking water!

Reducing your cistern's capacity

The first thing to do then, is to reduce your cistern's capacity to six litres (your friend can let go of the float now). There are a number of devices around which can do the job – the most famous being the 'hippo', which is available from www.hippo-the-watersaver.co.uk

But if you're impatient like me, you can always make your own.

A used, half litre bottle of water (or whatever) can be refilled with tap water, and placed in the bottom of the cistern. This is accurate and safe. You might want to look at using several bottles to measure out the amount you require. 'Cisterns installed before 1993 use nine litres per flush but can still be perfectly effective with six or seven' (www.cambridge-water.co.uk). So if your cistern is nine litre capacity, then you'll need six half litre bottles to reduce the capacity. It's that simple.

Be careful when you do this though, as the items in your cistern can easily be damaged or dislodged whilst adding your containers. It can also be quite a narrow space and you may find that the water bottles won't quite fit. If this is the case, then go for the hippo, or one of those provided by the water companies.

Other options

It would be nice, of course, to replace your toilet with a low flush version, but this would be costly overkill to simply save water! If, however, you do need to swap your toilet at any stage, it makes good sense to get a low flush model and then all this jiggery-pokery won't be necessary.

If you do have the money to invest, a rain harvesting system can provide the six litres of toilet flush, to completely replace this usage of clean, drinking water.

Baths and showers

Baths use 90 litres of water, whereas showers use only 30 litres, so definitely take a shower, not a bath. Power showers are to be avoided, as they can use up nearly as much as a bath.

If your shower is electric, and your hot water is from a carbon neutral source (such as a solar panel), then you may want to get a mixer shower fitted. This way you can have the best of both worlds – minimum water usage, heated by a carbon neutral source.

Another way to save even more water is to fit your shower with a low flow showerhead. You can ask for more information at your local plumbing or DIY store.

Washing machines

Most washing machines consume around 50 litres or more per load, so if you're thinking of getting a new model, or replacing your current model with a more efficient one, it is worth looking at how much water each one uses. A good list of comparisons can be found at www.waterwise.org.uk

The features of a decent A-rated washing machine are quite impressive. Many will allow you to select a maximum temperature or spin speed. They also often have very short programs, so for loads which just need to be freshened up, you can use the minimum amount of water (and energy). Do bear this in mind if your washing machine is up for renewal.

Brushing your teeth

Don't leave the tap running! You can just put the plug in and use a shallow amount of water. You can always rinse your mouth out either with a couple of swigs from the tap or from a glass of water.

As we've seen in the figures above, it's the difference between 10 litres and one litre of water.

CONCLUSION

Handling your own water supply and disposal is very expensive and takes a certain area of land, especially the handling of sewage. To do this job properly would take a purpose-built house such as that built at the Hockerton Housing Project or CAT in Wales. The prospects for fitting sustainable systems to existing housing are not good.

Having said this, there is likely to be a certain amount of waste in any system, so you can still have a look at how you use your water, and how it can be improved, most notably by looking at your toilet flush.

After looking at conservation opportunities around the house, the next change you could make is to install a water butt for watering the garden, and so on. These are widely available and relatively easy to fit. They also have the advantage of being exempt from any hosepipe bans!

If you do have money to invest in your water system, it is possible to implement a rainwater harvesting system which can primarily be used for flushing your loo, although this is likely to cost over £2,000 and take decades to pay off.

Beyond this you are looking at large, radical installations, such as a composting toilet or a reed bed. Such a change to your home (and possibly lifestyle) is going to cost a similar chunk to the rainwater harvesting system, and will require an area of land to be turned over to this purpose.

So for many of us, it's probably best to be economical with the water we get, and be thankful for the system we already have in place!

5

Transport

How our transport system stops relying on fossil fuels will be one of the stories of our generation. It is a surprising fact, unthinkable to some, that children being born now will never drive a petrol car. Fossil fuel depletion is such that within five to 10 years it will be far too expensive to drive using petrol, let alone 20 years.

If this seems unlikely, consider industry insider Matthew Simmons. He used to be energy advisor to George W. Bush, and now chairs a large investment bank specialising in energy investment. He is convinced that the price of oil will be over $200 per barrel by 2010, and places huge investments accordingly. Imagine how much oil will be by 2020... Dozens of books have been written on fossil fuel depletion, and yet it still seems to be largely unknown. *The Party's Over* by Richard Heinberg (Clairview Books 2007) is a good place to start if you want to find out more.

Overwhelmingly, our largest use of oil is for transport. Richard Pike, chief executive of the Royal Society of Chemistry, put this usage at 74 per cent. With oil fields around the world, including Britain's North Sea oil fields, in terminal decline, our transport system has to change. The big question is what we replace oil with. Unfortunately, there is no easy answer. The alternative fuels which are all currently vying for our attention, especially in the media, are:

- biodiesel
- straight vegetable oil (SVO)
- ethanol
- electricity
- hydrogen.

Currently, there seem to be no plans to completely replace our fossil fuel inputs, but to add a blend of 5 per cent biofuel to 95 per cent fossil fuel. This goes along with the government's Renewable Transport Fuel Obligation, which is aimed at having 5 per cent all road vehicle fuel from renewable sources by 2010. This is in answer to the European Union Biofuels Directive, which aims for similar results.

INPUTS

BIODIESEL

What is biodiesel? Essentially it is a replacement for diesel, but from biological ingredients. It should be usuable in an unmodified vehicle which runs on diesel.

The key here is 'unmodified'. The whole infrastructure we currently have in place can remain untouched, from the pump to the vehicle. The only change would be in the actual manufacture of the fuel.

Although many diesel engines will run perfectly well on biodiesel, some engines are safer to run on a blend of biodiesel and standard diesel, with some manufacturers being so cautious as to endorse only a 5 per cent *blend*, that is 5 per cent biodiesel to 95 per cent standard diesel. Blends such as this are classified by their percentage, so 5 per cent biodiesel is B5. Biodiesel without any standard diesel would be B100 (100 per cent biodiesel). It is the B5 blend which is currently available at many filling stations around the UK, *not* B100.

Advantages

Pure biodiesel, i.e. B100, has the advantage that it is produced from organic material, rather than crude oil. This means that much of the carbon emissions produced by the fuel are already part of the carbon cycle. It tends to be mostly carbon neutral and hence sustainable. As long as a vehicle is able to operate using such a fuel, then there is no reason why driving can't be carbon neutral. This is a far cry from our petrol-head present.

B100 can be grown and processed anywhere there is adequate farmland, thereby eliminating the highly political supply shocks that have thrown the world into turmoil in the past. Just about any country in the world could produce this fuel, and run vehicles.

In addition it is a biodegradable product, so there is no issue of pollution from fuel spills. No longer would tanker accidents cause massive environmental damage, as the stuff would simply return to the carbon cycle.

Disadvantages

Sounds perfect doesn't it? But there's always a catch.

Although some older vehicles, especially larger diesel vehicles such as trucks or trains, are more suited to running on B100, many current vehicles won't run on a 'pure' biodiesel. This is why only a blend is available at the pumps. So although Britain's current car fleet may need to be adapted to pure biodiesel, it may yet prove useful for running our infrastructure and possibly our public transport.

Recall that most biodiesel available at the pumps is only B5. It is still 95 per cent standard diesel. So how much are we actually gaining here? Of course, where biodiesel is available it should still be used, as it is still reducing the amount of carbon produced. However, it is a far cry from being carbon neutral.

We use too much to replace

Another big drawback to biodiesel is the capacity of oil that can be grown, compared with the number of cars currently on the road. George Monbiot, in his article 'Worse than Fossil Fuel' (6 December 2005) says:

> 'In 2003, the biologist Jeffrey Dukes calculated that the fossil fuels we burn in one year were made from organic matter "containing 44×10 to the 18 grams of carbon, which is more than 400 times the net primary productivity of the planet's current biota". In plain English, this means that every year we use four centuries' worth of plants and animals.' (www.monbiot.com)

Does this mean that we can't sustainably run cars on biodiesel? Well some of our cars can be run on biodiesel. What it does mean is that the scale of our current usage of fossil fuels is so grotesque that there is no way we can hope to replace the fuel for them all. How much fuel could we replace? In the same article above he says there is enough waste cooking oil in the UK to meet one 380th of our demand for road transport fuel.

One 380th, that's around a quarter of a per cent. So I guess we won't be needing that extra lane of the M1 after all...

Environmental impact

But surely we could switch more crops over to oil-producing ones? That's exactly what's happening at the moment, although less in Britain than in other countries. According to a report from Friends of the Earth, the creation of new oil-palm plantations in southeast Asia is causing massive deforestation. Millions of hectares of forest have been cleared in Sumatra aand Borneo, with millions more being planned in Malaysia and Indonesia. This is likely to lead to the extinction in the wild of species such as the orangutan as well as others such as the Sumatran rhinoceros and tiger. Beyond this, many thousands of indigenous people have been kicked off their land, with hundreds being tortured when they resisted.

So there's the rub – biodiesel is causing deforestation. Undoubtedly some of our vehicles could, and should, be converted over to B100. Tractors, buses, trucks and trains all make good candidates for conversion. Not only is it sustainable, but gives better security of supply. But to try to replace *all* our fuel use with biodiesel could cause a lot more trouble than it's worth.

How can I use it?

As noted above, biodiesel is available at the pumps of some petrol stations. However, as this is only a B5 blend, it may be worth ordering B100 from a mail order company. Whether your car is OK to run on B100 though is another matter.

One internet source (www.biodieselfillingstations.co.uk) claims that diesel cars built between 1990–2004 should be fine to run on 100 per cent biodiesel, with a one-off fuel filter change after the switch has been made. Cars built after 2004 should run on a 50 per cent blend. It also warns that some biodiesels, those made from waste cooking oil, will freeze in winter. To avoid this issue, it recommends a 50 per cent blend during the colder months, or biodiesel made from rapeseed oil as this doesn't freeze.

Biodiesel also has a quality specification called EN14214. This gives a certain guarantee of quality. It is recommended that you look for this standard when buying biodiesel.

Very few car manufacturers will endorse 100 per cent biodiesel. Again, according to www.biodieselfillingstations.co.uk:

> 'The companies that have approved 100 per cent biodiesel are VW, Audi, SEAT and Skoda. They have approved all their cars built between 1996 and 2004 on 100 per cent use of "RME" Biodiesel (biodiesel made from rapeseed) providing it meets the specification DIN41606 (which was later replaced by EN14214).'

Apparently, some new cars can even be provided with a warranty for 100 per cent biodiesel, although this does need to be requested from the manufacturer. To be safe, you should contact your car manufacturer, or least look them up on their website. There are also a number of enthusiasts out there who can point you in the right direction. For a list of available outlets in the UK, go to www.biodiesel-fillingstations.co.uk/outlets.htm

Alternatively, biodiesel in a variety of blends can be bought by mail order. See 'Useful Information' at the back of the book for more details.

For detailed information about how biodiesel is made, you should look no further than the excellent book *From the Fryer to the Fuel Tank* by J. Tickell (ECo-Logic Books 2000). This carries straightforward instructions on how to make your own biodiesel, although this is not a weekend project by any stretch of the imagination! But if you are serious about producing your own biodiesel and are willing to invest in the equipment necessary, then this would be an ideal place to start.

Straight vegetable oil (SVO)

At the 1900 World Exhibition, one of the original engines which was presented ran on unmodified peanut oil. (Although whether it was Rudolph Diesel himself or the French Otto Company that presented this particular engine, seems to be in dispute.) The main reason that petrochemical diesel became the choice for such engines was a matter of economics, rather than environmental factors. As the years have passed, these factors have changed and now it seems that we have come full circle.

Advantages

One big advantage of using SVO over biodiesel is that there is no processing involved, other than the processing of the plant into vegetable oil in the first place. This means that it is available 'off the shelf' to us, the general public. This is a tremendous advantage in itself, and allows for even easier supply as there is no need for the SVO to be sent to a plant to be processed into biodiesel.

Disadvantages

SVO cannot be used in an unmodified engine. Ever since the decision was taken that the fuel would be petrochemical diesel rather than an organic oil, manufacturers have naturally tuned their engines to perform according to the fuel for which it was intended. The main difference between SVO and diesel is that SVO is many times thicker than diesel. This can result in clogging engine parts, thick deposits and ultimately engine failure. These are not trivial problems, but thankfully they can be overcome. However, the vehicle in question must be modified. In the case of biodiesel the fuel is adapted; in the case of SVO the vehicle is adapted.

SVO also carries with it some of the same pluses and minuses as biodiesel, since they both have the root source of vegetable oil. So they both contribute less emissions, both are biodegradable and both, unfortunately, contribute to deforestation. The main difference with the two is that the fuel has not been processed when using SVO, but has been when using biodiesel.

How can I use it?

Can I use SVO in my unmodified diesel car? Some commentators seem to agree that a straightforward blend of 5 per cent or a little more, can be used in unmodified vehicles. One professional convertor, writing on www. dieselveg.com says:

> 'Mixing a small amount of veg oil to an unmodified diesel is, however, undoubtedly beneficial. Five per cent would probably not hinder combustion and would aid fuel system lubrication. There would also be an improvement in emissions, similar to that of the same bio-diesel mix which is widely sold at the pump.'

According to this source, there shouldn't be too much trouble with putting 19 litres of diesel in your tank, followed by a litre of sunflower oil straight out of the supermarket! **However this is at your own risk. Some cars are better suited to SVO than others**. If you are unsure whether you can use a blend of SVO in your car, check first with the manufacturer or a qualified mechanic. Also bear in mind that you may *breach your warranty* if you use any fuel other than that specified. (See SVO and the law on page 65 for more information.)

100 per cent vegetable oil

What about pure vegetable oil? Can I use that in my diesel car? Well, there's no short answer to that question other than *probably not*.

Straight vegetable oil (SVO) is much thicker than diesel. In order to burn properly, it needs to be in a fine spray, much like diesel. This is where the problems start. Unless the oil and/or the engine are warmed, which thins the

SVO, then you can't get a proper combustion. This is why an unmodified diesel trying to run on SVO will have cold start problems.

Problems such as clogged injectors can occur, but the main problem is that of starting up. When the SVO is cold, it causes undue pressure on the injection system. The cost of a failure can be your engine. However, once many diesel engines have warmed up, SVO can be substituted for diesel. For this reason, there are two main methods of converting a diesel car to run on SVO.

The two tank system

This involves having two fuel tanks, one for diesel and one for SVO. The fuel line is then split between the two and a switch governs which type of fuel is used. When starting, and just before stopping, diesel is used to prevent any start-up strain on the injectors. Then, when the engine is warm enough, the driver can switch over to SVO. When you come to finish your journey you will also need to idle on diesel for a short while to ensure that only diesel is in the system for the next start up.

The heated fuel system

This system involves heating the vegetable oil so that it has similar properties to diesel, and hence avoids the cold start problem. This has the advantage that only one type of fuel is required, SVO, so it is a truly carbon neutral vehicle.

Unfortunately I can't dive into a full, technical analysis of how such a conversion can be made. This is a huge area and several books have been written on this subject alone. If you are interested in making such a conversion yourself, two good books to find out more might be *From the Fryer to Fuel Tank* by J. Tickell and *The Edge Of Veg* by S. Helbig. For the technically astute, these books go into the hows of running diesel engines on SVO in great detail, explaining not just how to make a conversion, but also the principles behind such a conversion.

Several companies can also provide you with SVO conversions or simple kits to help you get started. Details are available in 'Useful Information' at the back of the book.

SVO and the law

Hang on, isn't using vegetable oil to run your car illegal? Not necessarily. If you wish to use vegetable oil as a fuel, or sell it as such, then you are liable for fuel tax. As long as you pay this tax, you are not in breach of the law. And since 30 June 2007, provided you don't use more than 2,500 litres of vegetable oil per year, you are exempt from duty. If you do go over this threshold, you will need to contact Customs and Excise and arrange to make quarterly fuel tax payments on the amount that you use.

However, according to the Revenue & Customs Brief 02/07 (issued on 5 January 2007), tax on small producers may be dropped completely, which might apply to anyone buying SVO for personal fuel use. However, this was only a proposal, and at time of writing, was yet to be confirmed.

If you are in any doubt as to whether you are liable to fuel tax, you are urged to contact Customs and Excise. Remember: if you use vegetable oil as a fuel in any quantity and don't register, then you may be in breach of the law.

ETHANOL

What is ethanol? Well if you've ever enjoyed a glass of whisky, then you are already familiar with it. It's commonly referred to in the UK as alcohol, and it's the same substance that's found in alcoholic drinks. Although it is possible to make ethanol from a petrochemical process, what we are interested here is bio-ethanol – that made from an organic source, typically sugar cane, switchgrass or corn. And, like alcoholic drinks, it is produced by yeast fermentation and then distillation. The only additional step before it can be blended with petrol is dehydration.

Like biodiesel, ethanol is often used in a blend with petrol and has a similar classification system, but instead of a 'B' for biodiesel, we have 'E' for ethanol, e.g. E10 is 10 per cent ethanol and 90 per cent petrol. E100 would be pure ethanol.

Advantages and disadvantages

Like SVO, pure bio-ethanol is a fully carbon neutral fuel. Provided that the energy used for powering a production plant is carbon neutral, then there is no reason why such a fuel can't be sustainable. Brazil is leading the way in ethanol production, mainly from sugar cane. All cars by law must be able to run on E23 or better.

But, like SVO, it cannot work in an unmodified engine. That is why most countries in the world, such as Brazil and the USA, use blends. In Brazil, all cars must be capable of running on a 25 per cent ethanol blend, and requires a similar blend for its fuel. Some states in the US require the fuel sold to be anywhere up to 10 per cent. Because so many countries require cars to run on ethanol blends, it is often speculated that all cars can run on blends of up to about 30 per cent to avoid having two sets of parts – ethanol blend, and non-ethanol, but this is not known.

Ethanol is corrosive and in high concentrations can damage some vehicle parts. Hence, only blends are typically allowed. A higher blend, E85, is sold at some pumps in the USA, but it requires a vehicle that has been especially adapted to run on such a fuel.

Although ethanol is carbon neutral, the emissions it creates are only marginally less polluting than burning petrol.

Environmental impact

Another disadvantage of ethanol is that it creates competition for land use. In a similar way that biodiesel may cause the extinction of orangutans in the wild, it has been argued that growing crops for ethanol production may cause food to become more expensive.

In a presentation at Downing Street, Richard Pike stated that: 'to achieve the 2010 EU 5.75 per cent biofuels target would require 19 per cent of arable land to be converted from food to biofuel crops.'

Clearly ethanol, like biodiesel, will never be able to replace our current transportation needs, and can only make a contribution. In Mexico, protests have been held about the dramatic increase in the price of tortillas, due to US corn being diverted to ethanol production. Over time, this problem will worsen, and already commodities such as corn and sugar are rapidly gaining in price.

How can I use it?

Britain seems to be somewhat behind the times when it comes to ethanol production, or rather the British government is behind the times. While countries like Brazil have replaced 40 per cent of their oil use with ethanol, Britain's attempts barely register. The first UK bio-ethanol plant will come into production at some time in 2007, and should hopefully provide a supply of E5 at the pumps. According to Envocare, the availability of ethanol at time of writing stands as follows:

'In the UK, in 2005, tax concessions for ethanol encouraged a minor shift and a 5 per cent ethanol mixture entered the retail market. A firm called Greenenergy pioneered this and Tesco have been reported as the retailers (mainly in SE England), the ethanol source being Brazilian sugar cane. The real motivation may be cost (although the reduction in price to the UK customer is small) but even so that is no bad thing. In 2006 another supermarket, Morrisons, started selling E85 bio-ethanol in East Anglia.' (www.envocare.co.uk/ethanol)

So ethanol is gradually becoming available, but it will be quite some time before it is available to all. The first bio-ethanol plant, from Green Spirit Fuels, will begin production in 2007.

Ethanol and your car

Can I use it in my car? Generally speaking, an E5 blend can be used by most petrol vehicles, but this should always be checked out with the manufacturer. The E85 blend, however, requires a specially designed vehicle: the Flexible-Fuel Vehicle (FFV). These are cars with a specially-designed engine, which can run on two different fuels; typically high ethanol blends, or petrol, with separate fuel tanks for each fuel.

Although only a small number of manufacturers currently produce cars compatible with E85, this number is growing all the time – so if you would like to make the change check around to see what's available.

Even then, bear in mind that supply of E85 fuel is sporadic in the UK at best. Really, unless you happen to live near to an adequate supply, then there's little point seeking out an FFV for your driveway. The only way this situation will change is if industry or government decide to change it.

ELECTRICITY

It's like something out of science fiction isn't it? A quiet car, with no emissions. And provided that the electricity is carbon neutral, then the car will be as well. This seems to shift the emphasis away from the vehicle and back to the energy production itself, as discussed in Chapter 3 – Electricity. There seems to be much fierce debate about at the moment regarding just how easily Britain could convert its fleet over to electricity. Not only would the vehicles themselves all need to be converted, but perhaps the national grid itself would have to be adapted as well, to handle the extra load from all these cars. This in turn asks where all this extra electricity would come from.

Types of electric car

Electric cars have been around for quite a while, but have mainly been concept cars rather than a practical alternative. However, as more and more people choose to go carbon neutral, electric cars are becoming a serious choice rather than the exclusive domain of milk floats and golf carts.

There are two types of electric car available today:

■ electric car

■ hybrid car.

The difference here is that while electric cars are 100 per cent battery operated, hybrids also use a petrol engine alongside, so that you are not entirely dependent upon the batteries. Petrol of course is hardly carbon neutral.

There have also been many criticisms made of some hybrids in recent years. These have included the high proportion of time that the engine is in use, rather than the electric batteries, as well as the high energy cost of manufacturing them in the first place. These advanced vehicles make use of advanced wiring and electronic components, which all push up the energy cost.

Recently, a new type of electric car has wandered slowly onto the market: the plug-in hybrid. This type of car has increased batteries, which allow it to be run on an electric input, charged straight from the grid. However, it still has the petrol input which allows it to make long journeys. Unfortunately for us here in the UK, this next generation of cars may be another year or two away.

Advantages and disadvantages

There are a number of factors which have traditionally been associated with electric vehicles of all types, and they tend to centre around how electric cars store their energy – the batteries.

The first issue here is range. Many older electric cars would probably only just about manage a modest commute on a full charge, but advances have been made in recent years, with some batteries boasting as much as 300 miles on a single charge. However, with increased range does come increased cost. Indeed, the batteries are often the most expensive part of the car, such that some manufacturers will actually lease the batteries to you at a cost of several hundred pounds per year.

The perks of running on electricity

This starts to sound expensive, until you realise the flip side of this is just how cheap it is to recharge your batteries compared with filling up your fuel tank. Remember that you pay no tax on electricity, compared to over 62p on a litre of unleaded! Also, electric cars are exempt from road tax, so this does need to be factored into your decision.

In London, it has been much publicised that not only are electric cars exempt from the congestion charge, they also get free parking and, in certain special bays, there are free recharge points. Now obviously, this would only benefit a small percentage of people living in Britain, but if you are one of them, then this might be worth looking into.

No support

As far as flexibility is concerned, electric is probably one of the best choices. However, it's important to remember that there are virtually no mechanics out there who will maintain an electric car. This means that you will have to do it yourself. Like many renewable options, the infrastructure isn't in place.

Final considerations

If you didn't already know, most electric cars are not performance models – they are slow! 50mph is fast for an electric car. So if you need to race up and down the country, an electric car is not for you (although there are a few electric sport models).

One final point worth bearing in mind is that unless the electricity you use to charge your car is carbon neutral, then neither is your electric car! This seems such an obvious point, but it should be raised. Using standard electricity from power stations burning gas or coal is no better than running a petrol car.

How can I use it?

For once, this is a straightforward question to answer – simply buy an electric car. Before taking the plunge though, it is worthwhile checking out how each model stands against the others, particularly when it comes to the batteries. Questions such as whether they are owned or leased, how long they are likely to last, and how much they might cost to replace, should all be asked and investigated.

Some well-known electric car retailers are listed below in 'Useful Information', although sadly the choice in the UK is somewhat limited compared to the selection available in the US, for example.

HYDROGEN

Hydrogen is everywhere. To make your own, all you need is water and electricity. When burned to produce energy it produces only water vapour – no carbon emissions or greenhouse gases at all. What could be a better source of energy for running vehicles than hydrogen?

Unfortunately, the reality is that hydrogen is not actually a *source* of energy at all. Due to inefficiencies, more electrical energy has to be put in to create the hydrogen than can be drawn out by burning it. It is effective only as a *carrier* for energy, and then at a substantial loss. This means that the hydrogen must be created in the first place, although the opportunity does exist to create this hydrogen using a carbon neutral source, such as a wind turbine.

Hydrogen is still very much a pipe dream and will probably never see fruition as a mainstream fuel. As a practical fuel for use by you or me, it doesn't even make it to the starting line.

Advantages and disadvantages

The main advantages with hydrogen, as we have seen, are that it is clean and relatively easy to create using electricity. Unfortunately, this is where hydrogen's big advantages end, and its problems start.

The first big disadvantage is that it is only useful as a fuel if it is firstly compressed. None of the other fuels we have looked at have this requirement. It needs to be compressed at the point where it is created, then transported along each stage in the supply chain using tanks which can handle compressed gas. This includes the tanker trucks, the filling station and the final vehicles themselves. This limits how much fuel can be carried in a vehicle, as the tank does need to be quite large. As such, there is currently no infrastructure in place in the UK for hydrogen vehicles, and probably never will be.

Cut out the middle man

Another major issue with hydrogen is that the hydrogen is created using electricity in the first place. It is then injected into a fuel cell in a vehicle, which then creates electricity to power the vehicle. When newer and more efficient batteries are coming onto the market all the time, why do we need hydrogen as the middle man? This introduces tremendous inefficiencies, converting back and forth from one medium to another, especially when we already have an electrical infrastructure in place – the national grid.

In short, hydrogen is an immature and tremendously expensive alternative technology. It is often limited to pilot programmes such as a two-year project which successfully ran two London buses on hydrogen fuel cells. Although there is no technical reason why some vehicles can't be run on hydrogen fuel, the cost is prohibitive.

How can I use it?

You can't, unless you have a vast fortune you are willing to spend on obtaining an appropriate vehicle and the necessary equipment to manufacture your own hydrogen.

OUTPUTS

As we've already mentioned, the outlook for replacing our current transport usage in a carbon neutral fashion is dim to non-existent. Eventually we will all need to power down to a greater or lesser degree. This is the political hot potato that no politician is willing to discuss. Our energy-hogging lifestyles are completely unsustainable, and sooner or later will begin to slide. Even if one of the alternative energies mentioned above were taken to a national scale, it would only be able to provide for a fraction of the population.

The only real alternatives for travel are by car sharing, scaling down, or walking or cycling.

CAR SHARING

Cars are perfectly capable of carrying five people instead of one, for very little extra fuel. Car share schemes are actually already in place in many work places, and there are several dedicated websites where you can register. To find your nearest, go to www.carshare.com and click on your region.

> One of the quickest ways to halve your fuel bill, and your carbon emissions from travel, is to share with a friend.

Ask around at work, or set up a discussion group on your network to help potential car sharers meet up. It really couldn't be simpler.

Public transport is also a potential way of sharing vehicles, but on a much bigger scale. Buses, trams and trains are all ways of sharing the cost and emissions of travel. Despite this, very few government subsidies flow to public transport companies, with the result that it is still often cheaper to drive to work than to get the bus.

Finally, getting goods delivered, rather than picking them up yourself, is also a method of sharing, since each person is effectively sharing the delivery van. This includes supermarket delivery schemes and local box schemes as well as the more obvious items, such as furniture.

Scaling down

There is still an awful lot of waste in our transport system. Many people still drive large, inefficient vehicles, when a smaller vehicle would satisfy their needs. One of the main reasons behind this of course, is that cars are status symbols. When did you last see the prime minister riding a scooter? Nor will we ever. Cars are directly linked to prestige in most people's minds to such an extent that they will gladly sink themselves into debt in order to drive a more expensive car. This attitude is one of the main barriers to scaling down our vehicle use.

Beyond this mental shift, it is a simple exercise to trade down to a smaller, more economical vehicle, even a carbon neutral vehicle. I heartily applaud the recent tax hikes for wasteful vehicles, and personally I would ban them altogether.

Self-powered – walking or cycling

Walking, riding a bike, even riding a skate board, is self-powered transport, and completely carbon neutral. This won't always be desirable, or even possible, but where a healthy walk or bike ride is an option, it should always be used.

Conclusion

For the next few years at least, there are carbon neutral options available for almost any travel needs, except flying. As fossil fuels deplete, however, options such as biodiesel and ethanol will become far more mainstream, for purely economic reasons. However, these solutions will create tremendous pressure on the environment as more land is lost to nature, and converted over to farming, to ensure a steady supply of biofuel.

In the long run, there really is no alternative to reducing consumption. This won't be voluntary; it will be forced upon us by the realities of supply and demand. Britain has been spoilt for years with huge supplies of cheap oil. Those years are about to end.

6

Food

INPUTS

According to the National Farmer's Union, 'UK food transport created 19 million tonnes of carbon dioxide in 2002 alone, ten million of those being emitted in the UK itself. That figure represents almost 2 per cent of the UK's total carbon emissions and 8.7 per cent of emissions from the country's roads'.

Just think how much oil and gas goes into simply having an apple in your fruit bowl. It's grown in a foreign country using artificial fertilisers made from natural gas, pesticides made from oil and mechanised farm machinery running on oil. It is flown or shipped thousands of miles, then carried by truck to a supermarket, which the customer drives to, and brings home in a plastic bag made from oil.

According to Defra (www.defra.gov.uk), in 2005 agriculture in the UK produced 85,000 tonnes of nitrous oxide and 873,000 tonnes of methane, which are believed to be worse global warming gases than carbon dioxide. When you include the 19 million tonnes of carbon dioxide emitted transporting food, it soon becomes apparent why food is such a big subject when it comes to climate change.

We all have to eat, but our current methods of industrial farming are fossil fuel intensive and this isn't sustainable. So what can we do about it?

BUYING LOCAL

And I don't mean the local supermarket! Wherever you live there will be farm shops, or farmers' markets. This drastically cuts down on transport, and consequently the impact on the environment. It also helps to support local farms and businesses, so effectively sponsoring the good guys.

Most of us do need to use the supermarket, so whenever you can, buy British. This is really just an extension of buying locally. And if possible, make use of supermarket delivery schemes – this is effectively car sharing, since a number of households have shared the journey of one van.

> Also, many farms nowadays have box schemes in their area, particularly organic.

This kills two birds with one stone – a local producer as well as delivery.

Also keep your eye out for neighbours round and about who grow their own; they may be willing to sell you some of their produce for a small sum. There are no end of people with fruit trees in their gardens who neglect to harvest the fruit each year. Even if they haven't put a sign out inviting you to buy it, why not ask anyway? If you offer to buy fruit from someone who has plenty to spare, they'll probably just give you a couple of bagfulls.

Also, don't neglect any local farms where fruit is bought on a 'pick your own' basis. This can work out exceptionally cheap and of course cuts down dramatically on your food miles. With just one trip you can often return with carrier bags full of fruit very cheaply.

BUYING ORGANIC

To make artificial fertiliser requires plenty of fossil fuels. In the introduction, we saw that in the US it takes 10 calories of fossil fuels to make one calorie of food. This figure is likely to be less in the UK, but still quite high. Organic food uses none of this, cutting down on emissions considerably.

CUTTING DOWN ON DAIRY AND MEAT

Although dietary requirements should always be considered, it is true that most commercially available dairy and meat, which isn't farmed organically, does have a high embodied energy. This is the energy it takes to make it in the first place, which is mostly obtained from fossil fuels either directly or indirectly. However, the amount of embodied energy will vary widely depending on the producer.

Becoming self-sufficient

Growing your own food

Wouldn't it be fantastic to have all your food in your back garden? You'd know where it came from, what pesticides had been used on it and no food miles! Of course to grow all your own food you'd need considerably more land than the average back garden, and a good deal of time. But that doesn't mean it shouldn't be done. Again, it is simply a case of doing *something*. If each family only grew ten meals' worth of potatoes this year, it would make a big difference to the carbon emissions of this country. And it is very satisfying to eat your own produce, and gives a sense of independence. (See 'But I haven't got room!' on page 91 if you don't have your own garden, or if it's very small.)

Vegetables

Why not turn just one border over to vegetables? This small area could then be part of a simple crop rotation: potatoes, legumes, brassicas, root crops. If nothing else, it will teach you the basics of vegetable gardening, a skill which is gradually being lost from our collective mindset as farming becomes more industrialised over the years.

Why not start with the humble potato? Our family grew our first potatoes by accident when we threw some potato peelings in a small border at the end of our yard. A few months later we noticed these huge, leafy growths – potato plants. We pretty much guessed when to pull them up, and lo and behold we had home-grown potatoes. This is what set me thinking about growing vegetables. I'd never done any gardening before, but here I had grown my own potatoes with very little effort.

Of course if you want consistently good results when growing vegetables, it is best to follow time-honoured techniques. And if you don't yet know your brassicas from your legumes, you really need to get a book specialising in the subject. *Growing Vegetables* by Tony Biggs is a good place to start. It includes information on when to prepare the soil, how much lime, compost or fertiliser to use for each crop, and how to select an appropriate variety for growing.

Over the years to come this activity will become less the activity of enthusiasts, and more a fact of life. As our fossil fuels head into the final stages of depletion and artificial fertilisers start to soar in price, so too will our food bills. Growing your own vegetables will become a simple matter of economics.

Fruit

You don't have to just grow vegetables, of course. Many fruits can also easily be grown in a British garden. These have the advantage of taking up less room than vegetables, and in many cases are less work. A blackberry bush in your garden, for example, once it has reached maturity, will provide you with a crop year after year and requires little weeding or compost. Britain can support a surprising number of different fruits which have often been dismissed due to our overcast, wet climate, such as grape vines. But if the right variety is selected, vines can be grown in Britain, and in quantity!

Essentially, for British climates, when selecting a species, you want to go for an early fruiting variety, so that it can make the best use of what sunshine we get. Also, look at how long it takes a plant to mature from planting, before it begins to provide a crop. Plum trees, for example, mature quite early on from when they are planted, and within only a few years can begin to provide fruit. Our vine was fruiting while it was in the pot the first year!

Milk

How about owning your own cow for milk? Just kidding! But there was a time when everyone owned a goat, as cows' milk was just too expensive to come by. This practice, and owning other animals like it, was the reason why the village green became common. Although folks often didn't have the land for grazing their own animals, or it wasn't practical (goats will eat your washing off the line if they get the chance) they still needed a place for their animals to graze, hence they had a communal piece of land. It was a bit like an allotment for animals.

Keeping a goat won't be possible for most people. It really depends on how independent you want to be with your milk supply, how much room you have, and how much time you have to look after it. Obviously land is an issue here, as goats do need to be housed as well.

> The big advantage of goats, and the reason they have been farmed at all stages of British history, is because they can eat almost anything and turn it into milk.

As anyone who has ever kept a goat will attest, they will eat whatever they can find. This is both a blessing and a curse!

You should check the deeds or leasehold agreement for any land where animals will be kept, in case you are in breach of such an agreement.

It can be a complex business keeping a goat. They need land for exercise and grazing, and adequate housing. Attention needs to be paid to their diet, as goats eat large quantities of roughage, usually in the form of hay, and they also need concentrates for good milk production. Goats are also herd animals by nature and much prefer to be in a group.

If you are lucky enough to be able to keep a goat, then bear in mind that it is one of the few ways that an ordinary householder may be able to secure their own milk supply. Also bear in mind that milk can be easily turned into cheese or yoghurt for consumption. Also bear in mind that a goat can be readily turned into meat!

Eggs

Keeping your own goat is a little far-fetched for most folks, but up to half a dozen hens in a backyard house and run is feasible. A good house will be fox proof and have nest boxes at the end. Hens are relatively simple to look after, they can survive on a wide variety of foods and if properly looked after should provide you with a good supply of fresh eggs.

If permanently positioned, however, the hens will soon dig up and muddy the area. Hens can be incredibly destructive! This is one of the reasons why free range chickens are unsuitable for most gardens – they will destroy vegetables and plenty of other plants which are there.

During the Second World War, hens were rotated around the garden with the vegetables. In the winter, the hens were moved on to the vegetable patch to get rid of insects and weeds, and to manure it ready for the next year.

Although I heartily applaud the free range method of chicken farming, it does need to be thought through carefully. A simple house and run will probably be sufficient (and practical) for most householders.

To begin with you will need to buy a small hen house with a run, and just a few hens. Two should be sufficient to get started. A good house will have nest boxes at the end, where the hens can lay from the inside, but with lids so that the eggs can be easily collected from the outside. Since we're talking about Britain here, ensure that the hen house is well insulated in the winter (usually with straw).

> **Coops, hens and feed can be bought over the internet.**

Some good sites to look at are www.pandtpoultry.co.uk, www.omlet.co.uk and www.ideas-4-pets.com, to name but a few. Initially you will need to pay out for the equipment and the birds, but once you are set up you should soon have free eggs!

As with keeping any animal, care and attention needs to be given to their feeding and general health.

Hens can be fed simply on grain and kitchen scraps if needs be, but this may not result in a fully balanced diet, with a resulting low yield in eggs. Typically, the diet is supplemented with specialised pellets, or they can be wholly fed on a bought feed, designed for egg layers, although this can work out quite expensive. But, like goats, hens can eat a huge variety of food, including grass cuttings, acorns and beech nuts.

Keep an eye out for disease, especially lice and mites to which they are prone. Most problems can be prevented by simple cleanliness, keeping food and drink containers clean and by changing the straw and sawdust regularly. To keep down lice and mites, use a dust for the purpose (such as Diaton), dusting the birds and coop regularly. The same company that sells you your coop should be able to provide you with the right equipment and consumables.

What you do next with your hens depends on whether you want them for breeding for chicks, or for the Sunday roast. Either path is beyond the scope of this book.

Rabbits

Rabbit farming? It may surprise you to know that during World War 2, in addition to hens and vegetables, it was common practice to keep rabbits – not just for the meat, but also for the fur. They are another animal that is hardy, easy to keep and easy to breed. Once again, they can be fed on what is available. Although rabbit meat isn't to everyone's taste, it was once common fare (as can be seen from the breeds of dog that have arisen over the years specifically for the hunting of rabbits and hares).

Getting started

To get started with keeping rabbits, all you will need is a couple of reasonable sized hutches, and a breeding pair. Preferably, the hutch should have a run attached to it, similar to the setup for chickens. The big problems with rabbits seem to be overheating in the summer and disease. So when siting a rabbit hutch, it is preferable to have one that's in the shade somewhat. Also, cleanliness is essential for preventing disease. You will need plenty of hay and sawdust for bedding, and this will need to be changed on a regular basis.

Rabbits are traditionally fed on oats, bran mash, greens, roots and hay, but they can also be fed on a wide variety of garden weeds.

> **If you have a run which can be moved around, then take advantage and move it around your lawn, keeping it neatly trimmed!**

I have heard of some rabbits tunnelling out of moveable runs, but most folks don't seem to have a problem with this. Another advantage of the moveable run is that less cleaning is required, and the rabbits will readily fertilise whatever ground they are moved to.

Breeding

Once you start breeding your rabbits, you will want to have extra hutches on hand. Although some breeders advocate keeping the buck in with a doe, this can cause fights. It is best if mature rabbits (any older than 8–10 weeks) are kept with their own sex. This means that you will need additional hutches as any kits mature. When you are ready to breed your rabbits, put a single doe in with a single buck, *and not the other way around*. As soon as they have mated, move the doe back to her own hutch for her pregnancy. Once the young have weaned from the doe, then move them into separately sexed hutches as per above, and then butcher at 8–10 weeks or move them into their own individual hutches for further breeding.

Another bonus of keeping rabbits in your garden or shed is the prodigious amounts of manure they produce! These are perfect for your composter, or can be buried nearby to your vegetables. You may want to have a raised hutch with a slatted floor for easy collection, not unlike the chicken coop.

Butchering animals

Firstly, my apologies to the vegetarians and vegans who are reading this, as well as anyone who keeps rabbits as pets. Since this section may not apply to you, you may want to skip it.

Even if you are intent on breeding and slaughtering animals for meat, you should give thought to your neighbours, or anyone else who might be offended by your actions. In today's society there is often considerable emotional distance between the animal and the plate, and even meat eaters can be shocked and upset when it is done in plain view. So do be sensitive to those around you when killing an animal.

Of the animals mentioned here, only goats may require professional assistance. For small animals such as chickens or rabbits it should be a simple exercise to convert them into meat joints. The best way to go about your first butchering is to get an experienced helper to talk you through it. If you don't know anyone who has the knowledge, you might enlist the help of your local butcher. Even though it can seem a messy business the first time you gut a rabbit, it can give you a tremendous sense of independence. You now not only have the means with which to breed your own beasts, but also to butcher them as well – you *are* self sufficient. This is a major step on the road to sustainability. Although the basic steps for butchering any animal are slaying, gutting, skinning and jointing, it is beyond the scope if this book to instruct you in this process. A good book such as *The Complete Book of Raising Livestock and Poultry* should be able to provide you with simple written instructions.

> **The most important point is that the animal is despatched in the most humane and hygienic way possible.**

Once again, do remember to be as discreet as possible and show consideration to your neighbours. They might not be as excited about your efforts to become carbon neutral as you are!

But I haven't got room!

This is a perfectly natural response. Many of us haven't got more than a small garden, others a yard, yet others, a flat! So unless you are lucky enough to live on a farm or smallholding, you will have to economise on space. Some of the advice offered by the practices adopted during World War 2 can be useful, and you may be surprised what can be done in such a small space.

At first glance, a yard may seem to be a case for no hope, but this is far from the truth. Many yards are paved only with slabs, in which case the slabs can be cleared in small sections to make way for your vegetable garden or chicken run. If the yard is concreted and cannot be pick-axed up for any reason, then you may still be able to reclaim it, using rows of heaped compost. Lacking any soil, you'll need as much as you can gather and the rows of soil will very quickly become depleted. This doesn't mean it can't be done, only that your highest priority task is to accumulate compost (see 'Outputs' below) in order to create your own topsoil. You may want to purchase some topsoil or compost to get started, but this isn't essential.

As well as adding your own top soil in a yard, you should also consider growing food in containers. Many vegetables, and even some fruit bushes, can be grown in large containers. However, you will have to pay particular attention to the quality of the soil, as it will have a limited capability of replenishing itself and could quickly become exhausted.

Allotments

The next best thing you can do for growing your own vegetables is to get an allotment. Even in the centre of large cities, there are usually allotments with spaces available and as long as you don't cause a nuisance to your neighbours, you can grow anything. I even know of one family in our village who have planted fruit trees on theirs – an orchard allotment.

> For those who want to get started with their own vegetables (or fruit) but lack the land or simply don't want to turn their rose beds into a turnip patch, this is definitely the way to go.

Many of us do have a garden, but keep it for leisure. Children and pets are obviously another restriction which may cause damage to a garden given over to vegetables.

If there isn't an allotment nearby to you, is it possible to purchase your own land, or group together with like-minded neighbours and form your own allotment scheme? Land is relatively cheap in many areas, but it won't stay that way for long. Fossil fuel depletion will mean that land becomes at a premium once more. If petrol is replaced with bio-diesel, how much extra land will be needed to grow crops for the oil? As wood replaces natural gas or coal for heating, how much extra land will be needed for forestry and logging? So look around, and see if there are any unused pieces of land which you may be able to buy up cheaply.

Finally, you can always work alongside your local farmers. Harking back once again to World War 2, it was not uncommon practice to keep an animal on a nearby farm. An arrangement was reached with the local farmer whereby a portion of the animal's produce was given over to the farmer, or the farmer could be paid for the animal's upkeep. As long as a local farmer agrees, there is no reason why this practice can't be resurrected. My wife's gran kept a pig at their local farm so as to help out with the rationing at the time. Talking to local farmers about your plans is a good way to set out, and may result in a useful pooling of resources. Whether your plans call for a whole field, or simply a corner of one for your chicken coop, it is likely that a farmer can lend a helping hand.

HUNTING AND FORAGING

In our modern times, hunting and trapping seem to have fallen out of favour. It is often viewed as morally (or legally) wrong to go out and hunt for food, be it with dog, gun or trap, but perfectly fine to buy your meat from the supermarket. We live in times where almost any meat may be had for a reasonable price here in the West, and there is little need to hunt for food. Perhaps this is the reason why many seem content to besmirch these activities, because they feel there is no need. As the price of fuel rises dramatically, the need for local meat will rise with it. And remember that these activities are largely carbon neutral.

Meat farming, really, is little more than convenience hunting. Our ancestors ate a much wider variety of animals because of the expense and scarcity of bought meat. Only the local landowners would have had the wealth for regular supplies of meat. In our local area alone pheasants, pigeons, rabbits, hares, even rooks were eaten, and a wider variety of fish such as pike and eel.

Hunting is also much harder to go about these days, since very little land is left for common use, and hunting with dogs is now banned. That said, hunting with shotguns and air rifles is still possible, provided you have the land owner's permission. The same is true for trapping and fishing, and many water courses do remain in the public domain, provided you hold a current rod licence.

Another more overlooked source of meat is roadkill. Obviously, you will want to be quite picky about what you take though! There is a big difference between a hedgehog squashed flat, and a rabbit at the side of the road which is still warm. Remember that the most important step when finding an animal at the side of the road which is already killed, is to get it home and drop the guts out as quickly as possible to avoid tainting the meat.

Foraging

Another widely ignored practice is that of gathering your own food from your local neighbourhood. It is quite amazing what can be found in the hedgerows, from the more obvious food such as blackberries, to the less obvious, such as nettles for nettle soup. Crab apples, elderflowers, elderberries, hawthorn flowers and birch sap can all be used to make wine. Hawthorn berries, rowan berries and others can be made into jams and crab apples are prized for their pectin. In spring, even the leaves from lime trees can be eaten like salad leaves, or in a sandwich – lime trees are to be found in almost every park. And in the autumn, keep your eyes peeled for chestnuts to be roasted.

These are some of the more obvious foods that grow wild, many of them close to your home.

> There are literally thousands of plants which can be used either simply to flavour our food or drink, or be eaten in their own right (such as nettles and blackberries).

Of course, you need to make sure that you have correctly identified any wild food that you pick, as some plants and berries can be poisonous.

So why not get out and about in your local area and see what food is growing? Just a few meals a month locally will once again make a difference to your food miles and it may encourage you to view your local plant life with renewed interest. If you are not sure which plants can be eaten, then why not get a book or two on the subject? A good title is *Food for Free* by Richard Mabey.

All year round there will be at least one or two plants in season which you can eat, but obviously in the winter there will be slimmer pickings – which brings me to the next subject.

PRESERVING FOOD

In this age of supermarket food where self sufficiency been replaced by dependency on fossil fuels, how many of us know how to preserve food? When food couldn't be had all year round, every household knew how to preserve the harvest they had, as their food supply depended on it. Canning, pickling, smoking, salting, drying and freezing can all be used for preserving foods. Nowadays we leave this up to the large corporations.

As you begin to explore the methods above for obtaining more and more of your own fresh food, you'll soon find yourself with more than you can eat before it goes off. Blackberries, for example, can start going furry after only a couple of days. They last longer in the fridge, but only up to about a week at most. So if you've come back from a foraging expedition or a pick your own farm with a carrier bag full of blackberries, you can save some for jam. All you need is a recipe, which can be gleaned from a book or the internet in just a few minutes, some sugar and some jars. The only bought ingredient, to ensure a good set, is pectin. This is a naturally occurring ingredient, found in apples. So apple and blackberry jam, for example, doesn't need any pectin.

If you want to go further than this, or preserve other items such as vegetables, you'll need to investigate further. A good book to get started with is *Canning and Preserving for Dummies* by Karen Ward. You'll also need to invest in some extra equipment, but don't let this put you off. You'll also want to start saving your own jars, rather than putting them in the recycling.

Blackcurrant jam

Here is an example recipe for blackcurrant jam that will make about 10lb (4.5 kilos). Because blackcurrants contain their own pectin, you won't need to add any, so the only added ingredients here are water and sugar. The end product can be stored in recycled jam jars.

   1.8 kg (4lb) blackcurrants

   1.8 lt (3 pints) water

   2.7 kg (6lb) sugar

Boil the blackcurrants in the water and simmer for half an hour. Meanwhile, warm the sugar in a bowl in the oven for 15 minutes at 110°C/ 225°F/gas mark 1. Then stir the warm sugar into the hot fruit and water until dissolved. Boil again until the jam sets.

To see if it is set, put a teaspoon of jam on a cold saucer for a minute or two, then push it to see if it wrinkles.

Beyond simple jams, you can preserve practically anything by one of the methods mentioned. So if you're already growing your own greens and have too much to eat, then why not go about canning some?

Meat is best frozen, smoked, salted or dried. Most folks have a freezer nowadays, so if you've managed to catch a rabbit, for example, then once it's been gutted, skinned and jointed, simply pop it in the freezer until you're ready for that rabbit in cider recipe! But other methods of preserving aren't that complicated. In Africa, for example, giraffe meat is preserved by drying – small strips are simply cut off then put onto a thorn bush to dry in the sun, cooking and preserving in one stroke. Giraffe jerky!

> **In Britain, the best ways to preserve meat are freezing and salting.**

As the cost of electricity goes up, however, our generation may be the last to take freezing for granted. Salting was commonly used and curing salt is still available although not so easy to get hold of nowdays. It is normal table salt, but with sodium nitrate or sodium nitrite added to help keep the meat for longer. One old recipe for preserving a ham recommends using two pints of salt. No wonder salt used to be a valuable commodity! Typically, meat would have been kept in a salt box, or the fridge, for three weeks, then hung. This would then keep for months or even years. There is often a reluctance to have a go at preserving meat, as food poisoning can occur if the process is botched. It is good to be cautious, but as long as you follow a suitable recipe and use the right ingredients, there shouldn't be any problems. A good book to get you started is *Cold-smoking and Salt-curing Meat, Fish and Game* by A. D. Livingstone.

Preserving food can be a challenge, but also rewarding. It is not something that most people think of when they consider going carbon neutral, but it is a vital component in the long run. And if you can't face all those jars of jam you've made, they do make excellent gifts!

HOME BREWING

Save the world whilst drinking; it's almost too good to be true. If you think this isn't a contribution to going carbon neutral, consider the food miles in a single bottle of Australian wine. But most of us (me included at one time) would have thought nothing of trying an Australian wine over, say, a German wine. As we've previously mentioned, agriculture is perhaps one of the biggest culprits for carbon emissions, from artificial fertilisers, production, processing to transport.

So if making jams isn't your thing, how about making a few gallons of your own wine for a fraction of the price? While it's true that there is a fair amount of equipment needed to get started, this can usually be obtained quite cheaply second hand, as many people have some of this kit stowed away and rarely used. I was given half my kit by relatives when I got started and only really had to buy the disposables like yeast and campden tablets. Although yeast can be obtained naturally, it is best to start off with a bought yeast, which you can then make into a starter bottle. All you need to do then is to keep that bottle going. Even if you use most of it, it only takes a little yeast to multiply into a full colony, by giving it more fuel (usually fruit juice and sugar).

> **Wine is the most versatile of alcoholic drinks and can be made from almost any fruits.**

Blackberries, elderberries, elderflowers, raspberries, rose petals, oak leaves, nettles, crab apples, hawthorn berries and hawthorn flowers can all be made into wine. A bagful of the quantities can be easily obtained for free by taking a walk at the right time of year. Many such harvests go untapped in these abundant times, when at any other period of history before the oil age they would have been picked clean.

Probably the most costly ingredient for home brewing is the large quantities of sugar required for the yeast. This is best obtained by the sackful from a Chinese supermarket, or local wholesaler.

So as well as saving jars for your jam, you will also need to start saving bottles for your wine. If you can't save up too many in the time available, just ask your neighbours if they have any they can contribute. Luckily in our area, glass is separated out into its own box for recycling when put out for the weekly collection, so it is simply a matter of wandering down the street on a Wednesday morning and having a look.

OUTPUTS

COMPOSTING

Essentially this section deals with compost! You might argue that it also should cover sewage, since that's what food ends up as. But since the water bill covers the disposal of sewage, I've grouped that in the water section.

Waste food material is not the only item which can go into compost. Almost anything can go in which was recently living. The categories of compost material are:

■ greens

■ greens and browns

■ browns.

Greens

Greens are the ingredients that will get a compost heap going. They include materials with plenty of nitrogen such as grass mowings, any very young plant material, or nettles. They also include urine (to three parts water) and vegetarian animal droppings. Remember your chickens and rabbits? Even horse or cow manure will be suitable. Unfortunately, dog and cat poo is not suitable, as it apparently contains undesirable pathogens which are then carried into the soil. Although some authors suggest that these pathogens can be destroyed by the composting process, there is not sufficient evidence and information available.

Greens and browns

Most materials fall into this category and include kitchen scraps (excluding meat and bones), manure which is clumped into bedding, tea bags, damaged fruit and vegetables, even hair and feathers. These tend to provide the bulk of material that is to be rotted down and although it frequently has some nitrogen to get it going, the greens are usually needed as well.

Browns

If your heap consisted only of the materials above, it would compost quite quickly, but would soon become a wet, smelly, slimy mess! To balance this out, you need browns. These are harder materials which are more difficult to break down such as sawdust, cardboard, paper, straw, junk mail. They also include the tougher, more woody garden waste such as thick hedge clippings, twigs and tree cuttings. If you were to have too much of this material in your compost, nothing would happen at all! In one of my earlier attempts, I simply put a whole food box in the heap. When I came to mix it through a few months later, I found the cardboard box still intact! These 'brown' materials must be shredded up at least a little. Tear up boxes, and screw paper up into balls. Don't simply put your junk mail in as it comes – take out a bit of aggression on it! For tougher material, like woody clippings, you may need a shredder or an axe. A friend of mine used to run the mower over it!

Most problems with compost come from not paying enough attention to the *balance* of materials in the compost. Too much green, and it becomes too mushy, but too much brown and it will dry out and stall.

Getting started

The biggest problem with making compost isn't usually getting enough material, it is having the space. Get as big a bin as you possibly can. You may not believe it, but that bin will likely be full within as little as two or three months!

When it comes to getting a compost bin, don't rush out to your local DIY store.

> **Many local authorities are now offering very cheap compost bins in an effort to get more people to compost.**

Go to www.recyclenow.com where you can get them delivered. Site it away from the house, and have a little 'kitchen caddy' for day-to-day kitchen scraps. This saves constantly traipsing to the bottom of the garden for each small item.

If you're still not sure what to do, simply have a go! You will find opinions differ greatly on what can or can't be included in compost. Meat, fish and bones are the often hotly-debated items. Joseph Jenkins, in *The Humanure Handbook*, contends that *anything* can be composted (well, almost anything) and, as the book's name suggests, he is a fan of composting poo as well.

Joseph argues that materials on the 'banned' list *do* rot down if they are in a 'hot' compost heap, and that humanure combined with other ingredients is the best way to create such a 'hot' heap, encouraging these banned items to decompose quickly. If the heap is too cold then it tends to rot down too slowly which means that the items can stay there for longer, providing a food source for rats and other vermin.

Use your own manure? Well that's what's being recommended in *The Humanure Handbook*. Many composting toilets simply involve throwing in a handful of sawdust every time you go, which does make very rich compost. But if that's not your thing, then manure can always be sourced from rabbits, chickens or a local farmyard. These are your 'greens'.

Another item which causes controversy is weeds. Should they be composted, or will they and their seeds survive the process and go on to grow more weeds in your garden? 'Hot' compost heaps – those with plenty of greens in – should be virulent enough to kill off weeds and their seeds. However, if you're in doubt then burn any weeds and put the ash into the compost. (Ash from living materials is perfectly acceptable in a compost heap, but coal ash is not.)

> Home composting is one of the most overlooked and easy ways to start becoming carbon neutral.

If you use nothing else in this chapter, use this! If you already recycle plastics, cardboard and glass, then you begin to compost as well, you'll soon find that your landfill wheelie bin is practically empty! The only items left will be thin, plastic food wrappings that can't really be recycled, and any small food items you decide not to compost. For all those who complain about the smell of their wheelie bin, because it is only emptied once a fortnight, I say 'compost!'

7

Shopping

INPUTS

IS CARBON NEUTRAL SHOPPING ALWAYS ETHICAL?

Carbon neutral shopping is probably one of the most complex topics around. There are a number of reasons for this. First and foremost, just because an item has a small carbon footprint, it doesn't necessarily mean that it's ethical, an issue which is important to many people. *The Good Shopping Guide*, for example, lists categories such as pollution, nuclear power, animal testing, factory farming, workers' rights, irresponsible marketing, armaments, genetic engineering and political donations against each brand or company. None of them really cover the 'carbon cost' of the products involved, and conflicts can occur. For example, if a company abuses its workers' rights, but uses all renewable energy in its plants, should we buy their products or boycott them? What about nuclear power? It's low carbon, right?

It is because of knotty issues such as this that there can be no simple answers on what to buy and what not to buy. In order to get a clear view of what is going on behind the scenes of the manufacture of each item involved we need to do our own research.

Information tsunami

Another reason that it is difficult to know how to shop ethically is the sheer scale of the information involved. There are thousands of products and behind each product is a long and complex journey. For example, let's take a tin of beans from the local supermarket:

1. Beans (and other ingredients) are grown, then sent to processor.

2. Metal ore for the can is mined, then sent to smelters.

3. Metal ore is smelted, then rolled, then sent off to can makers.

4. Metal sheet is made into a can, then sent to processor.

5. A can of beans is made.

Even in this grossly simplified process, we can see that there are several companies involved, and at each stage of the process carbon emissions are released. Remember that much farming is done using artificial fertilisers, made using natural gas or coal. Smelting uses up huge amounts of energy. And at each stage of the process, the materials have to be transported, which I doubt is done using hybrid trucks!

Although some companies do provide information about their activities, in the form of environmental reporting, many more do not. Even then, the information provided is not in any great detail, certainly not to the degree where we will ever know the true carbon cost of even one can of beans, let alone a vacuum cleaner!

So what can I do?

What this section *can* do, is to give you some broad guidelines and some tools to go about your own further research.

PRINCIPLES OF CARBON NEUTRAL SHOPPING

Buying second-hand

So many things are easily available to buy second-hand. The more obvious places to look are charity shops and the small ads of your local newspaper. Newspaper ads are an especially good choice for bulky goods which need picking up, such as bikes, computers and TVs.

Car boot sales and markets are another area where second-hand goods can be picked up for a song. A fairly recent idea in Britain, car boot sales enable anyone to sell (almost) anything. This could count as inputs or outputs, depending which side of the stall you're standing on. More permanent markets can be a goldmine of second-hand items, especially books and tools. Periodic markets, such as farmers' markets, are also well worth checking out and often have a far wider range of goods than you might imagine.

Finally, there are online markets and recycling schemes, such as www.ebay.co.uk and www.freecycle.org.uk. The purist may argue that online auction schemes, for example, are far from carbon neutral as they need computers, electricity, and postage. This is all fair comment, but then this energy is probably much less than it would take to manufacture the items sold from scratch, so a saving is made.

Freecycle is one of the best ideas around for recycling unwanted items. Essentially, you sign up to the group in your area, then you receive a daily email listing items either wanted or offered for free. You simply reply and arrange for a pickup. It's like an online auction site, but for free! In today's digest for our area alone, there were offers of two duvet sets, glasses, ladies' clothes, pond plants, car seats, a fleece jacket, square torch batteries, a camping cooker, a soldering iron, a bunk bed, baby clothes, boys' clothes, a wall mirror, a bike and an inkjet printer! Imagine, if everyone was signed up to freecycle, how little landfill there would be.

> As long as you're not too proud to buy second-hand, this is one of the best ways to save money, and help reduce waste and unnecessary purchases.

There are plenty of perfectly serviceable items which are thrown away every day. This means that more items have to be manufactured to replace them, when in reality an item could have been passed on to someone else.

Buying British

This has already been mentioned in the food section, but it's important enough to be mentioned again. This reduces the distance an item has to travel. Even better than buying just British, is buying items that were manufactured locally, although this is harder to do for shopping items than for food. Even if a car factory is sited down the road from us, all the components and materials for that car were probably imported from the far corners of the globe before they got to the factory. This principle can be harder to uphold than it first appears.

Even if you can't buy British, then at least try to choose a country of origin that's closer by. Germany, for example, might be a better choice than China.

Buying sustainable products

This is the principle of sustainability. For example, always buy rechargeable batteries, rather than disposable. Although they both ultimately end up in the landfill (unless your council is a pioneer in this area, and some are), there would be far fewer if everyone used rechargeables. The Green Shop (www.green-shop.co.uk) stocks rechargeable batteries with a solar-powered charger.

For many items, admittedly, this can be hard to measure. For example, who knows how long a certain brand of kettle will last?

Another obvious item is cotton nappies, rather than disposables. The debate over disposables versus cotton nappies will probably rage for quite some time, with opponents of cotton nappies pointing out how much energy it costs to wash them, especially if tumble dried. But the fact remains that it is somewhat cheaper from birth to potty, if you shop around, and disposables do clog up the landfill, being made of plastic. About three billion nappies are thrown away in the UK every year and about 90 per cent of them end up in landfill. It is not known for certain how long it takes a nappy to rot down, but some sources say it could take hundreds of years.

For each item you use ask yourself if there is a reusable version of it. I use an old-fashioned razor, which takes razor blades, rather than buying disposables. If you look at each item you buy, there is often more opportunity in this area than there first appears.

Buying recycled

There's little point in recycling if you don't buy recycled items! Wherever possible it's important to buy recycled goods, such as paper.

Reconditioned goods are often overlooked. This can be a bonanza for electrical goods such as washing machines or fridge freezers. In many towns there are small workshops where worn-out goods are refitted to give them a new lease of life, then advertised for sale in a local newspaper. (Ideally, these would be reconditioned A+ appliances, but that's probably expecting a bit much.)

The 'Useful Information' section at the back of the book has a list of different recycled goods' suppliers.

Jumping up the supply chain

Before the era of the internet, goods traditionally went from manufacturer to wholesaler to retailer, with each one requiring transport, and adding on their own mark-up. This arrangement has begun to break down since the dawn of the internet, as it means that anyone can sell to anyone. But even so the supply chain is still there, and wherever we can bypass it, the better.

This includes buying items directly from wholesalers wherever possible, as well as farm shops and factory shops. This will reduce on transport as the items are carted from place to place, and possibly packaging as well. If you can buy goods in bulk, then so much the better. At the very least this will mean fewer journeys, and can mean less packaging in a lot of cases.

Less 'embodied' energy

Embodied energy means the energy it took to make something in the first place. In the case of the can of beans, the embodied energy is the energy it took to mine the metal, smelt it, roll it, make it and transport it to the shop. The embodied energy in a computer, for example, is even higher than that of a car!

Unfortunately, goods don't carry a label to tell us the embodied energy before we buy, so we have to guess. As a *very* rough guide, the more technically complex the item is, and the more heavy metal and plastic it contains, the higher its embodied energy.

GETTING THE FACTS

As previously mentioned, half the battle of shopping with an eye towards being carbon neutral is getting the right information. Unless you're actually buying second-hand or completely recycled goods, there will usually be a carbon cost. The challenge here is to reduce the cost to a bare minimum.

Listed below are a few tools you may find useful in deciding where to shop, and how to spend your earnings wisely.

Gooshing

The website www.gooshing.co.uk is not only a price comparison site, but also rates each brand automatically for its ethical credentials. Although this may not necessarily correspond with being carbon neutral, it may at least give you a start in the right direction.

The Good Shopping Guide

Updated regularly, this compact guidebook offers a summary of the major brands in each area. It is run by The Ethical Company Organisation, which also runs Gooshing. Although the focus is on ethical shopping as a whole, it also has a strong environmental theme throughout.

EIRIS

EIRIS – Ethical Investment Research Service (www.eiris.org). This company provides help and advice on ethical investing in areas such as pensions and trust funds. Pensions make up a significant sum on the financial markets. Why not investigate where your money is invested?

Trucost

Available online at www.trucost.com Trucost provides reports and services which rate companies on their environmental credentials, rather than simply broad ethics. This may help anyone who wants to minimise the carbon cost of their investments.

OUTPUTS

The principle of sustainability has always been echoed in the phrase 'reduce, reuse, recycle'. This simple mantra really carries all we need to know about our shopping outputs. Several of the possibilities have already been mentioned in Inputs, such as freecycle, and it is essential that we balance both sides of this equation. So if we receive an item from freecycle, then we ought to pass it back that way when we've finished with it, rather than tipping it.

So much of our way of living is disposable that it's become a mindset. As soon as you begin to question these habits, many new possibilities appear.

AVOIDING WASTE

Reduce

Reducing is a state of mind as much as anything, and it comes from looking at buying habits. The first way to reduce waste is to avoid buying something in the first place. But if you must buy an item, then consider how much waste is going to result from this purchase. This includes not only the item itself but any batteries, packaging, water it might use and so on.

One obvious area of waste is direct mail. If you would like to avoid unwanted direct mail, you can register with the Mailing Preference Service. You can do it online at www.mpsonline.org.uk, or write to Mailing Preference Service (MPS), DMA House, 70 Margaret Street, London W1W 8SS. Their phone number is 0845 703 4599.

Finally, you can avoid buying items by sharing them with neighbours. This might include vacuum cleaners, lawnmowers or other portable items. I've come across some neighbours who hire a carpet shampooer between them once a year, and share the cost. It's all a matter of using your imagination.

Reuse

We live in a disposable society, where items are often thrown away regardless of whether they have a use or not. Only when it starts to hurt the pocket do we realise that there is still some use left them.

Printer cartridges

For several years these were sold and thrown away without any recycling, until the price began to climb. Now we have refill kits which allow us to simply refill the cartridge (although admittedly they do tend to smudge after a few uses).

Cleaning fluids

The same applies to cleaning fluids, you can buy a large container and then refill it. If you must throw the original away, fill it with water first and use the diluted fluid – this works really well with washing up liquid.

Carrier bags

Reuse your carrier bags – they're perfectly serviceable for months, and a lot of places now offer a 'bag for life'. They can also be used as sandwich bags (as long as you know what's been in them!). And write your shopping list on a junk mail envelope.

Repairing

Repairing items also falls into this category. Sadly, the skills for repair are slowly disappearing. How many folks check if an item really has broken down, or if the fuse has simply blown? It can be fun to take an item apart and see if it can be repaired, or if it has completely burned out. Bikes, washing machines, fridges and other items can all be repaired if you are willing to spend the time to have a go. When I was a student in a shared house the washing machine broke down, and the Chinese students immediately took it apart to see what the problem was. Within a few days it was working again! This 'can do' spirit seems to have vanished from British mentality. I once had a friend whose job it was to replace broken video players on warranty for a high street retailer, and most of the time the problem was fixable with a screw driver.

And finally, if an item really has come to the end of its life, always salvage parts from it. At the very least, snip the plug off before you send it to the scrap yard. And if you know a local workshop that turns these items out, offer it to them for spare parts. Cut up old clothes for dusters. Squeeze every last drop out of the items you buy.

Recycle

Probably one of the most important and least used areas. In our affluent society plenty of serviceable items are sent to the scrap heap purely on grounds of fashion, or tattered appearance. Try selling it in the first instance, or giving it away on freecycle – the ultimate recycling bank!

There are also several schemes set up to recycle items back to the manufacturer, or to the developing world where even items like pens are in short supply. Mobile phones, computers, monitors, bikes, and a range of items can all be recycled rather than be dumped in landfill. See 'Useful Information' for more details.

Many local charity shops will accept books, CDs, videos, clothes and games, as well as a range of household goods. In addition to this, some local charities will often accept computers for use within the organisation, or accept other items for recycling in order to raise money for their organisation, so ask around.

CONCLUSION

Shopping, like food, is probably one of hardest areas to be specific about your carbon footprint, and it can be frustrating to buy a British-made item and not know how much carbon you've just saved.

Having said that, it's an area where we can easily make changes. We might not all be able to afford solar hot water, but we can all change where we go shopping, and we can all recycle.

So take a step back next time you're about to buy something, and look at how you can make a more carbon neutral purchase. Needs batteries? Buy some rechargeables. Can it be bought recycled? Or even second-hand? Take another look at your local area, and see what the shops have to offer.

It's surprising when you look at all the items you buy in a month to see just exactly how much of it ends up in landfill. If you can make just one or two low carbon purchases each month, it will make a big difference in the long run.

Every time you buy something, you are making a vote for that shop, or that website, or that manufacturer. The next time you buy something, vote carbon neutral.

Useful Information

Preface: Earth at Breaking Point

For help with setting up an Eco Team
www.globalactionplan.org.uk
Tel: 0207 405 5633

Clason, S. *The Richest Man in Babylon* (2007) www.bnpublishing.com

1 Getting Started

Statistics about the global atmosphere
www.defra.gov.uk/environment/statistics/globatmos/gagccukem.htm

CO_2 calculator (National Energy Foundation)
www.nef.org.uk/energyadvice/co2calculator.htm

Kunstler, J.H. *The Long Emergency* (2005) Atlantic Monthly Press, New York

2 Heating

Ground source heat pumps
www.lowcarbonbuildings.org.uk/micro/ground

Solar thermal hot water
www.lowcarbonbuildings.org.uk/micro/solartherm

Energy Savings Trust
www.est.org

3 Electricity

Low Carbon Buildings Programme
www.lowcarbonbuildings.org.uk

Permissions and approved components
www.greenenergy.org.uk/pvuk2/reference/grid_con/permissions.htm

Your Project
www.energy4all.co.uk/yourproject.php

Assessment and rating of noise from wind farms
www.dti.gov.uk/energy/sources/renewables/publications/page21743.html

Green tariffs – tariff types
www.energywatch.org.uk/help_and_advice/green_tariffs/tariff_types.asp

Appliances approved for funding
www.clear-skies.org/Households/RecognisedProducts.aspx

Approved installers
www.lowcarbonbuildings.org.uk/info/installers/find/installerfind

Wind speeds by area
www.dti.gov.uk/energy/sources/renewables/renewables-explained/
wind-energy/page27326.html

Energy Networks Association (for list of DNOs)
www.energynetworks.org
Tel: 0207 706 5100

Green Power Companies
Ecotricity
Axiom House, Station Road, Stroud, Gloucestershire, GL5 3AP
Tel: 08000 326100
home@ecotricity.co.uk

Good Energy
Monkton Reach, Monkton Hill, Chippenham, Wiltshire SN15 1EE
Tel: 0845 4561640
enquiries@good-energy.co.uk

Green Energy (UK) plc
6 Peerglow Centre, Marsh Lane, Ware, Herts, SG12 9QL
Tel: 0845 4569550
enquiries@greenenergy.uk.com/sellusenergy@greenenergy.uk.com

Small Turbine Companies
Eclectic Energy (Stealthgen)
Tel: 01623 821535
sales@duogen.co.uk

Renewable Energy (Swift Turbine)
Tel: 0115 353301
info@renewabledevices.com

Windsave
Tel: 0845 3904390
info@windsave.com

4 Water

Energy and sewage
www.parliament.uk/documents/upload/postpn282.pdf

Water calculator workings
news.bbc.co.uk/1/hi/sci/tech/5084234.stm

Rainwater harvesting and reusing grey water
www.cat.org.uk/information

Reducing water for flushing
www.hippo-the-watersaver.co.uk

Boreholes
www.h2oplc.com/bore_holes.htm

Using water efficiently
www.cambridge-water.co.uk/community/efficiency.asp

Ranking of washing machines
www.waterwise.org.uk/reducing_water_wastage_in_the_uk/house_and_
garden/ranking_of_washing_machines.html

Jenkins, J. *The Humanure Handbook* (2006) Jenkins Publishing, Grove City

5 Transport

The Energy Challenge – how chemistry can deliver
www.rsc.org/images/DowningStPresentation2_tcm18-59481.pdf

Running cars – fuel and conversion information
www.biodieselfillingstations.co.uk/approvals.htm
www.dieselveg.com
www.envocare.co.uk/ethanol.htm

Revenue & Customs information
http://www.hmrc.gov.uk/briefs/excise-duty/brief4307.htm

Suppliers of biodiesel
Pure Biodiesel Ltd
www.purebiodiesel.co.uk
cotswold.tours@virgin.net
Tel: 01453 872266

Eco Bio Fuels Ltd
www.ecobiofuels.ltd.uk
sales@ecobiofuels.ltd.uk
Tel: 01482 310147

Future Fuels
www.biodiesel-fuel.co.uk
Tel: 0845 22 22212

SVO conversions/kits
Biotuning Online shop selling parts to help assist in home conversions
www.biotuning.co.uk
mike@biotuning.co.uk

Dieselveg Ltd conversion company which also sells parts to assist in home conversions
www.dieselveg.com
info@dieselveg.com
Tel: 01902 450001

Goat Industries supplies parts to assist in home conversions
www.vegetableoildiesel.co.uk
paddy@goatindustries.co.uk
Tel: 01248 671982 (mobile: 07818 691255)

Smartveg conversion company which also sells parts to assist in home conversions
www.smartveg.com
fittingcentre@smartveg.com
Tel: 01235 850347

Electric car retailers
Elettrica UK
www.travelelectric.co.uk
sales@travelelectric.co.uk
Tel: 01425 402 579

GoinGreen
www.goingreen.co.uk
ask@goingreen.co.uk
Tel: 020 8574 3232

NICE
www.nicecarcompany.co.uk/home.html
theteam@nicecarcompany.co.uk
Tel: 0845 NICE CAR

Sakura
www.sbsbsb.com
sales@sbsb.co.uk
Tel: 020 8896 1133

Twike
www.twike.co.uk
info@twike.co.uk
Tel: 0770 7237070

Car share schemes
www.carshare.com

Tickell, J. *From the Fryer to the Fuel Tank* (2000) Eco-Logic Books

6 Food

Reducing food miles
www.nfumutual.co.uk/lifestyle/issue-one/reducing-food-miles.htm

Carbon emissions
www.foodcarbon.co.uk/carbon_emissions.html

Biggs, T. *Growing Vegetables* (1999) Mitchell Beazley, London

Thear, K. and Fraser, A. *The Complete Book of Raising Livestock and Poultry* (1988) Pan Books, London

Benson, R. *Ragnar's Urban Survival* (2000) Paladin Press, Colorado

Mabey, R. *Food for Free* (2007) Collins, London

Ward, K. *Canning and Preserving for Dummies* (2003) John Wiley & Sons, Chichester

Livingston, A.D. *Cold-smoking and Salt-curing Meat, Fish and Game* (1996) The Lyons Press

7 Shopping

Sustainable, eco friendly and fair-trade products
www.greenshop.co.uk

Retailers of recycled items
www.recycledproducts.org.uk

Network where members give things away to promote waste reduction
www.freecycle.org

Recycling organisations
Bicycles
www.re-cycle.org
Tel: 0845 458 0854

Mobile phones, PDAs, printer cartridges
www.actionaidrecycling.org.uk
Tel: 0117 304 2390

Computers
www.cksgroup.co.uk
Tel: 01993 411416
www.recommit.co.uk
Tel: 01722 339660

Suppliers of recycled goods
Guitars
www.simonleeguitars.com
Tel: 07976 751847

Paper, office supplies
www.greenyouroffice.co.uk
Tel: 0845 4564540
www.duraweld.co.uk
Tel: 01723 584091

Printer cartridges
www.cartridgeworld.org
Tel: 0800 1833800

Recycled video tapes
www.cva.co.uk
Tel: 01454 410255

Price comparison site, which also rates a brand's ethical credentials
www.gooshing.co.uk

Ethical Investment Research Service
www.eiris.org

Mailing Preference Service
www.mpsonline.org.uk

Rating companies on environmental credentials
www.trucost.com

Mulvey, C. *The Good Shopping Guide* (2006) The Ethical Marketing Group

Index

Printed in Great Britain
by Amazon.co.uk, Ltd.,
Marston Gate.